بسم الله الرحمن الرحيم

I LOVE ISLAM

2

CD Included

ISLAMIC STUDIES TEXTBOOK SERIES - LEVEL TWO

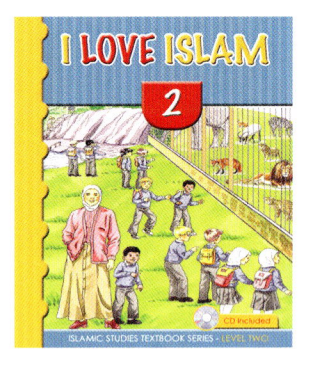

I Love Islam 2

بسم الله الرحمن الرحيم

In the Name of Allah, Most Compassionate, Most Merciful

I Love Islam © is a series of Islamic Studies textbooks that gradually introduces Muslim students to the essentials of their faith. It brings to light the historic and cultural aspects of Islam. The series covers levels One through Five, which are suitable for young learners, and it includes a student textbook and workbook, as well as a teacher and parent guide.

The Islamic Services Foundation is undertaking this project in collaboration with Brighter Horizons Academy in Dallas, Texas. Extensive efforts have been made to review the enclosed material. However, constructive suggestions and comments that would enrich the content of this work are welcome.

All praise is due to Allah (God), for providing us with the resources that have enabled us to complete the first part of this series. This is an ongoing project, and it is our sincere wish and hope that it will impact our Muslim children today and for many years to come.

Copyright © 2018 by Islamic Services Foundation

ISBN 1-933301-21-1

All rights reserved. No part of this publication may be reproduced or transmitted in any form or by any means, electronic or mechanical, including photocopy, recording, or any information storage and retrieval system, without permission in writing from the publisher.

Program Director *
Nabil Sadoun, Ed.D.

Writing Team
Aimen Ansari
Nabil Sadoun, Ed.D.
Majida Yousef

Reviewers and Advisors
Susan Douglass
Freda Shamma, Ph.D.

Contributors
Ummukulthum Al-Maawiy
Jaena Al-Mallah
Lana Baghal Dasti
Lena Dirbashi
Suzy Fouad
Hayah Sharif
Bushra Zawi
Menat Zihni

English Editor
Sumaiya Susan Gavell

Curriculum Design
Majida Salem
Nabil Sadoun, Ed.D.

Graphic Design
Mohammed Eid Asad

Illustrations
Raed Abdul Wahid
Sujata Bansal
Neha Firoze
Ramendranath Sarkar
Special thanks to: Goodword Books

Islamic Songs and Poems
Noor Saadeh
NoorArt Inc.

Photography
Al-Anwar Designs
Isam Alimam

PUBLISHER AND OWNER

ISF PUBLICATIONS

Islamic Services Foundation
P.O. Box 451623
Garland, Texas 75045
U.S.A
Tel: +1 972-414-5090
Fax: +1 972-414-5640
www.myislamicbooks.com

* Names are in alphabetical order of last names.

UNIT A

IMAN IN MY LIFE

Chapter 1	I Obey Allah: The Story of Prophet Adam A2
Chapter 2	I Think of Allah First A18
Chapter 3	The Sons of Adam A24
Chapter 4	My God Is My Creator A30
Chapter 5	I Trust Allah: The Story of Prophet Nuh A38
Chapter 6	Turning to Allah: The Story of Prophet Younus A48
Chapter 7	Taqwa: Allah Sees Me All the Time A62

UNIT B

I LOVE MUHAMMAD ﷺ

Chapter 1	Aam-ul-Feel: The Year of the Elephant ... B2
Chapter 2	Muhammad: The Praised Child B12
Chapter 3	The Orphan B22
Chapter 4	The Blessed Young Man B34
Chapter 5	As-Sadiq Al-Ameen: The Truthful, the Trusted ... B42
Chapter 6	The Happy Marriage B52
Chapter 7	Zaid Bin Harithah B58
Chapter 8	Prophet Muhammad Loves Children B68

UNIT C

BORN TO WORSHIP

Chapter 1	The Shining Treasures C2
Chapter 2	Zaid Learns How to Make Wudoo' C12
Chapter 3	Let's Pray! C20
Chapter 4	I Am Seven; I Pray the Right Way C30
Chapter 5	Thikr after Salah C36
Chapter 6	Du'aa: Ask, and You Will Be Answered C46
Chapter 7	Bilal Makes Athan C56
Chapter 8	I Fast in Ramadan................................. C68

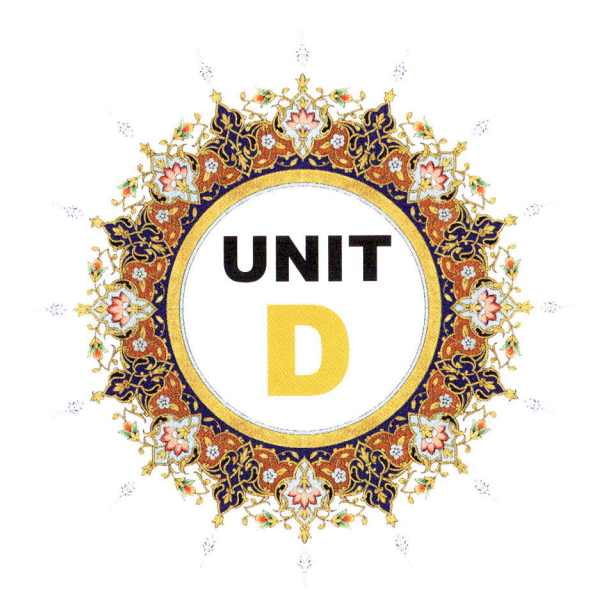

ISLAM IN THE WORLD

Chapter 1	It Is Eid! Allahu Akbar! D2
Chapter 2	Eid Around the World D8
Chapter 3	Masajid Around the World D20

UNIT E

MY MUSLIM MANNERS

Chapter 1	Who Is My Hero?	E2
Chapter 2	I Am a Muslim; I Am Honest	E12
Chapter 3	I Love My Family	E20
Chapter 4	I Respect My Teachers and Elders	E30
Chapter 5	Zaid and Leena Go to the Masjid	E40
Chapter 6	Learning Is First	E50
Chapter 7	My Muslim Room	E60

I Love Islam: Friends and Family

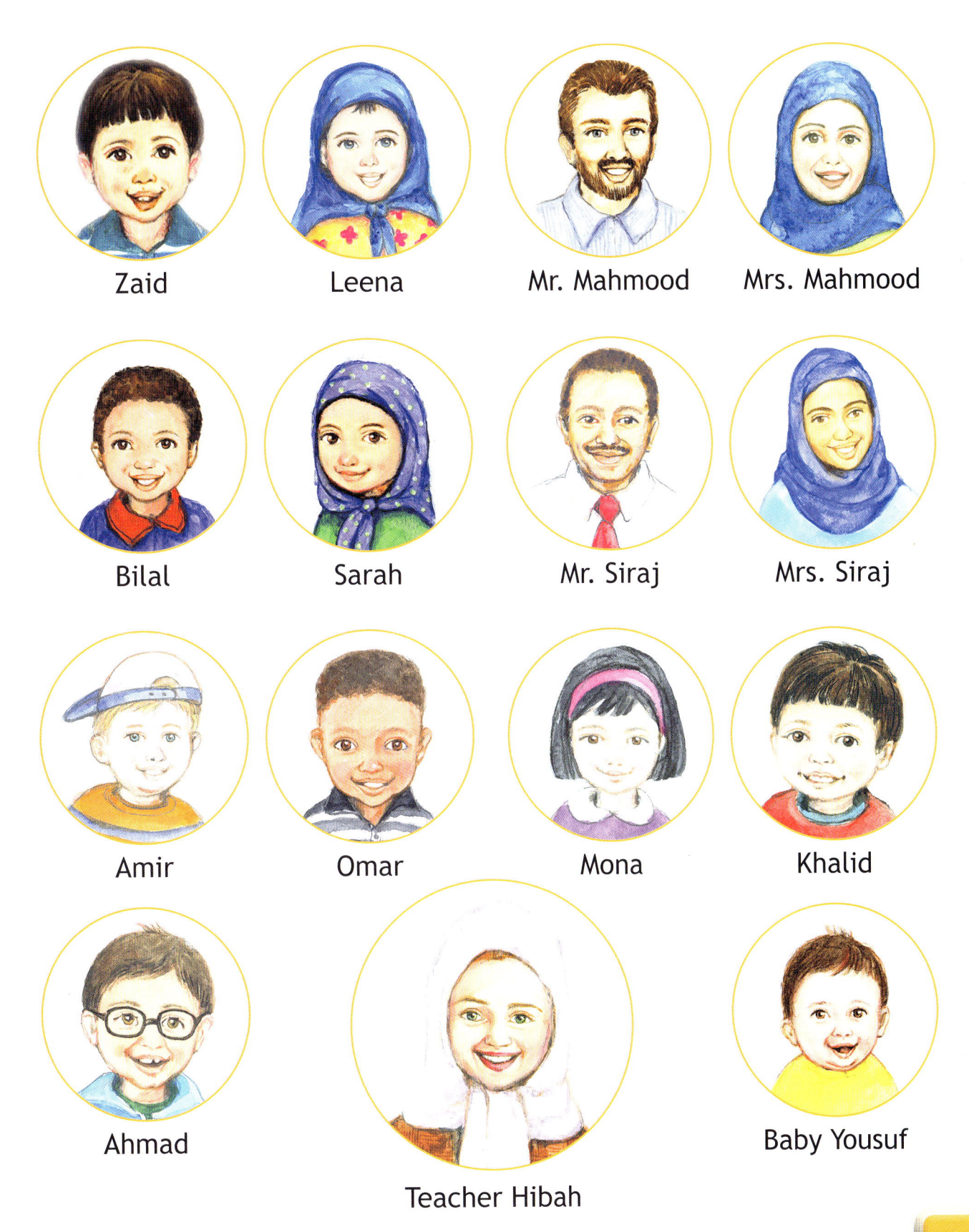

- Zaid
- Leena
- Mr. Mahmood
- Mrs. Mahmood
- Bilal
- Sarah
- Mr. Siraj
- Mrs. Siraj
- Amir
- Omar
- Mona
- Khalid
- Ahmad
- Teacher Hibah
- Baby Yousuf

ix

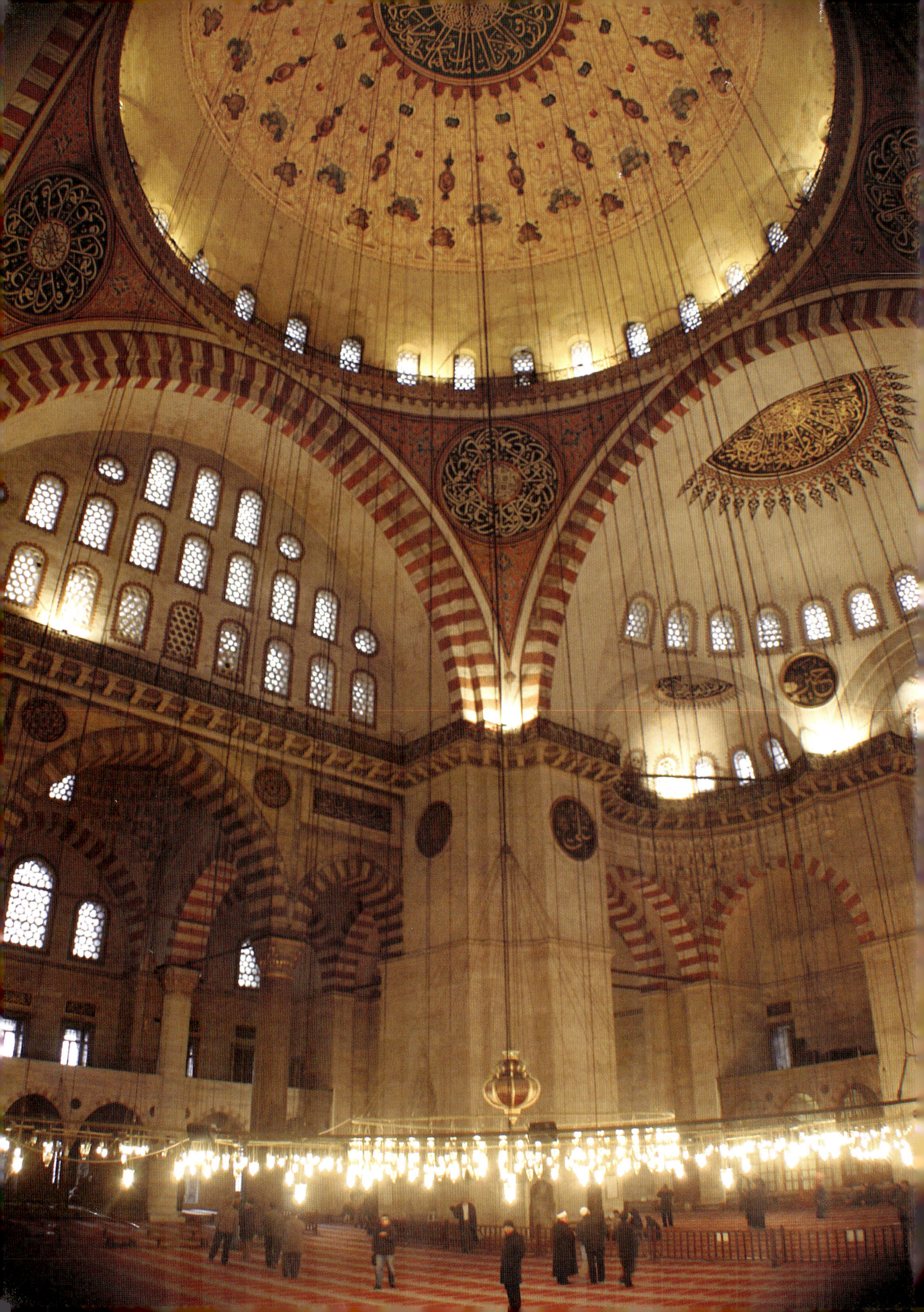

UNIT A

IMAN IN MY LIFE

Chapter 1	I Obey Allah: The Story of Prophet Adam A2
Chapter 2	I Think of Allah First A18
Chapter 3	The Sons of Adam A24
Chapter 4	My God Is My Creator A30
Chapter 5	I Trust Allah: The Story of Prophet Nuh A38
Chapter 6	Turning to Allah: The Story of Prophet Younus A48
Chapter 7	Taqwa: Allah Sees Me All the Time A62

UNIT A CHAPTER 1

I Obey Allah: The Story of Prophet Adam

questions?

1. Who made us?
2. Who should we always listen to and obey?
3. Who is Shaytan? Is he an angel?
4. Who is the first human Allah ever made?

word watch

Adam	آدم
jinn	جِن
Shaytan	شيطان
Iblees	إبليس
rajeem	رجيم
obey	يُطيع
Jannah	جَنّة
Jahannam	جَهَنَّم

Allah created the first human out of clay. He named him "Adam." **Adam** was the first man Allah ever made, so Adam didn't have a mother or a father.

He was also the first prophet. The story of Adam عليه السلام teaches us how important it is to **obey** Allah.

A2

A long, long time ago, before there were any people, Allah gathered all the angels. He told them to bow down to Prophet Adam, the first human, to show their respect.

All the angels bowed down to Adam عليه السلام except

IBLEES

Iblees was arrogant. He refused to bow down to Adam, because Adam was made of clay, and Iblees was made of fire.

Do you know what creatures are made out of fire?

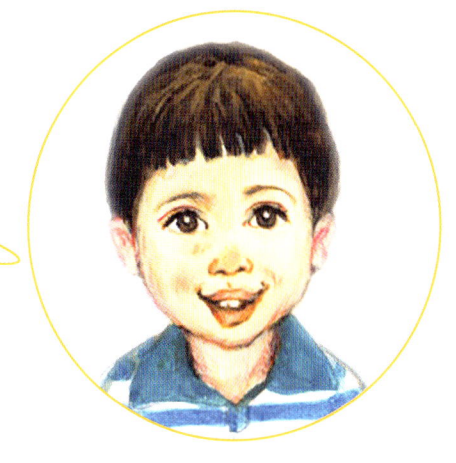

Jinn are made from fire. There are good jinn and bad jinn. Iblees was not an angel. He had been a good jinn, but he disobeyed Allah's order to bow down to Adam. This made Iblees a bad jinn. Iblees thought he was better than Adam.

A3

> How did Iblees dare to disobey Allah in such a bad way?!

What Iblees did was not smart. He made Allah very, very angry with him.

Allah told Iblees:

$$ قَالَ فَٱخْرُجْ مِنْهَا فَإِنَّكَ رَجِيمٌ ﴿٣٤﴾ $$

"Then, get out of here (Heavens) because you are rajeem (cursed and punished)." Surat Al-Hijr: 34

Allah sent Iblees out of Heaven and told him that he would live in Jahannam, or Hell after a while. Allah gave him a new name: **Shaytan**, or Satan. This meant he was away from Allah's mercy and that he would burn in Hell. Shaytan then promised to trick people to disobey Allah and do bad deeds so they would go to Hell like he would.

Ever since that day, Shaytan has tried to make people disobey Allah and do bad things.

Are we going to listen to Shaytan and do bad things?

NO! NO! NO!

Healthy habit

Whenever Shaytan tells you to do something wrong, or when you feel like being bad, you should say:

أعوذ بالله من الشيطان الرّجيم

"A'oothu billahi mina-Shaytan-ir-rajeem"

This means: "I ask Allah to protect me from the cursed Shaytan."

A5

A6

Allah taught Adam the names of everything. Adam learned everything he needed to know.

One day, Adam woke up from his sleep. He found a woman looking at him. Allah had created this woman from Adam's rib. She became Adam's wife. Some scholars say her name was Hawwaa', or Eve. The Qur'an and Prophet Muhammad ﷺ did not tell us what her name was.

Prophet Adam and his wife lived in Jannah, or Paradise. It was a beautiful place to live. There was a lot of food to eat and everything they needed.

Allah told Adam and his wife that they could eat anything they wanted. However, Allah ordered them NOT to eat from one fruit tree. Allah warned them that if they ate from that tree, they would lose Jannah. So, Adam and his wife obeyed Allah and did not go near the tree.

One day, Shaytan came to Adam and his wife. He told them that they should eat from the tree. Shaytan told them that if they ate the fruit of that tree, they would become angels and live in Jannah forever!

Shaytan Lied!

Allah had given so many trees to eat from, but they believed Shaytan. They ate some fruit from the forbidden tree. They disobeyed Allah.

> **Do you think they became angels?**
>
> **Do you think they lived forever?**

> **Did they stay in Paradise?**

NO!

Adam عليه السلام and his wife did not become angels. They did not live forever, and they did not stay in Paradise! Shaytan had tricked them! Allah told Adam and his wife that they had done something very wrong. They felt bad for disobeying Allah. They asked Allah to forgive them and be merciful and He did.

WORDS OF WISDOM
HOLY QUR'AN

سورة الأعراف

Surat Al-'A'raf: ayah 32

بِسْمِ ٱللَّهِ ٱلرَّحْمَٰنِ ٱلرَّحِيمِ

قَالَا رَبَّنَا ظَلَمْنَا أَنفُسَنَا وَإِن لَّمْ تَغْفِرْ لَنَا وَتَرْحَمْنَا لَنَكُونَنَّ مِنَ ٱلْخَٰسِرِينَ ۝

TRANSLITERATION

[32] "Qala rabbana thalamna anfusana wa-in lam taghfir lana watarhamna lanakoonanna min-alkhasireen"

TRANSLATION

[32] "They said: "Our Lord! We have wronged our own souls: If you do not forgive us and do not give us mercy, we shall certainly be losers."

Healthy h a b i t

Say: أستغفر الله العظيم

"Astaghfirullah"

This means: "I ask Allah to forgive me."
Ask Allah for forgiveness after every prayer, and whenever you can.

A9

Allah is **Al-Ghaffar & Al-Ghafoor**

الغَفَّار والغَفور

The All-Forgiving

Allah forgave Adam and his wife, but He sent them down to Earth.

Adam عليه السلام on Earth

Adam and his wife learned their lesson. Allah forgave them because they were sincere. They were truly sorry that they had disobeyed Allah and listened to Shaytan.

Allah sent them to Earth, far away from the easy life of Paradise. On Earth, Adam and his wife had to work hard. They had to look for food, and they needed to protect themselves with clothing and weapons.

They missed Paradise!

Allah made Adam the first prophet on Earth. Adam and his wife had children. They taught their children to obey Allah and worship Him.

Adam and his wife taught them to be good people so they would please Allah and go back to Jannah. Their children had children. Some of them were good and obeyed Allah. Many others listened to Shaytan and became bad.

> Allah forgave Adam and his wife because they were sincere. They felt truly sorry that they had disobeyed Allah. Allah made Adam the first prophet on Earth.

Nasheed

SHAYTAN Is My Enemy

Don't listen to the Shaytan!
He'll never be your friend.
Just read Qur'an, pray to Allah!
On that you can depend.
And if he whispers something
That's bad to do or say,
Just say these words "a'oothu billah,"
And he will run away.

The Shaytan....................
He'll never be your friend!

The Shaytan's like a stranger.
At first he may seem nice.
His talk is sweet, he offers treats,
But you must first think twice!
He'll whisper something softly,
"Don't mind your mom and dad."
But you must know this is not so,
All Muslims think it's bad!

The Shaytan...................
He'll never be your friend!
The Shaytan's very sneaky.
You hardly know he's there.
He's up and down, he's all around!
All Muslims must beware!
He'll whisper something softly,
"Don't read Qur'an or pray."
Just say these words "a'oothu billah,"
And Shaytan runs away.

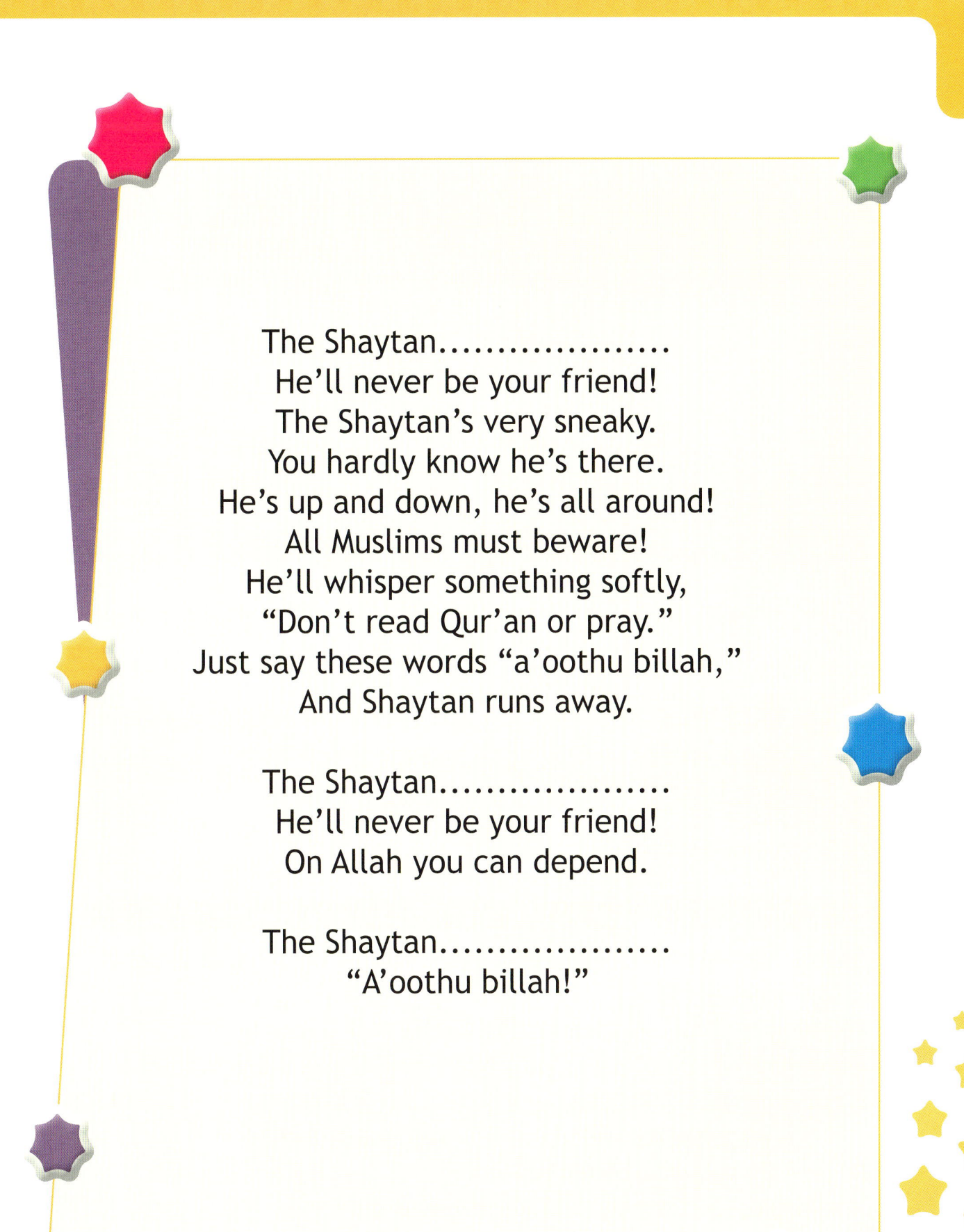

The Shaytan...................
He'll never be your friend!
On Allah you can depend.

The Shaytan...................
"A'oothu billah!"

Listen to this nasheed on *Track 2* of your CD.

WORDS OF WISDOM
HOLY QUR'AN

سورة طه

Surat Taha: 116-123

بِسْمِ ٱللَّهِ ٱلرَّحْمَٰنِ ٱلرَّحِيمِ

وَإِذْ قُلْنَا لِلْمَلَٰٓئِكَةِ ٱسْجُدُوا۟ لِءَادَمَ فَسَجَدُوٓا۟ إِلَّآ إِبْلِيسَ أَبَىٰ ۝١١٦ فَقُلْنَا يَٰٓـَٔادَمُ إِنَّ هَٰذَا عَدُوٌّ لَّكَ وَلِزَوْجِكَ فَلَا يُخْرِجَنَّكُمَا مِنَ ٱلْجَنَّةِ فَتَشْقَىٰٓ ۝١١٧ إِنَّ لَكَ أَلَّا تَجُوعَ فِيهَا وَلَا تَعْرَىٰ ۝١١٨ وَأَنَّكَ لَا تَظْمَؤُا۟ فِيهَا وَلَا تَضْحَىٰ ۝١١٩ فَوَسْوَسَ إِلَيْهِ ٱلشَّيْطَٰنُ قَالَ يَٰٓـَٔادَمُ هَلْ أَدُلُّكَ عَلَىٰ شَجَرَةِ ٱلْخُلْدِ وَمُلْكٍ لَّا يَبْلَىٰ ۝١٢٠ فَأَكَلَا مِنْهَا فَبَدَتْ لَهُمَا سَوْءَٰتُهُمَا وَطَفِقَا يَخْصِفَانِ عَلَيْهِمَا مِن وَرَقِ ٱلْجَنَّةِ ۚ وَعَصَىٰٓ ءَادَمُ رَبَّهُۥ فَغَوَىٰ ۝١٢١ ثُمَّ ٱجْتَبَٰهُ رَبُّهُۥ فَتَابَ عَلَيْهِ وَهَدَىٰ ۝١٢٢ قَالَ ٱهْبِطَا مِنْهَا جَمِيعًۢا ۖ بَعْضُكُمْ لِبَعْضٍ عَدُوٌّ ۖ فَإِمَّا يَأْتِيَنَّكُم مِّنِّى هُدًى فَمَنِ ٱتَّبَعَ هُدَاىَ فَلَا يَضِلُّ وَلَا يَشْقَىٰ ۝١٢٣

TRANSLITERATION

[116] Wa-ith qulna lilmala'ikat-isjudoo li-Adama fasajadoo illa Ibleesa aba

[117] Faqulna ya Adamu inna hatha 'aduwwul-laka walizawjika fala yukhrijannakuma min-aljannati fatashqa

[118] Inna laka alla tajoo'a feeha wala ta'ra

[119] Wa-annaka la tathma'o feeha wala tad-ha

[120] Fawaswasa ilayh-ish-Shaytanu qala ya Adamu hal adulluka 'ala shajarat-il-khuldi wamulkil la yabla

[121] Fa'akalaminha fabadat lahuma saw-'aatuhuma watafiqa yakh sifani 'alayhima miw-waraq-il-jannati wa'asa adamu rabbahu faghawa
[122] Thumm-ajtabahu rabbuhu fataba 'alayhi wahada
[123] Qala-hbita minha jamee'an badukum liba'din 'aduww-un fa-imma ya'tiyannakum minnee hudan faman-ittaba'a hudaya fala ya dillu wala yashqa

TRANSLATION

[116] When We said to the angels, "Bow to Adam," they bowed, except Iblees; he refused.
[117] Then We said: "O Adam! this is an enemy to you and your wife, so let him not get you both out of the Garden, so that you will live in misery.
[118] "There is here in it [enough food and clothes] for you not to go hungry nor to go naked,
[119] "Nor to suffer from thirst, nor from the sun's heat."
[120] But Satan whispered evil to him; he said, "O Adam! shall I lead you to the Tree of Eternity and to a kingdom that never ends?"
[121] They both ate from the tree, and so they became naked: they began to cover themselves with the leaves from the Garden. Thus did Adam disobey his Lord, and allow himself to sin.
[122] But his Lord chose him (for His Grace); He turned to him, and gave him guidance.
[123] He said: "Go down, both of you, all together, from the Garden, with enmity one to another. But if there comes to you Guidance from Me, whoever follows My Guidance will not lose his way, nor fall into misery.

ACTIVITY TIME

Keep a log for one week. Each day, write three good things that you did to please Allah, just like Adam and his wife. This way we can practice doing everything for Allah. We should remember Him all the time. The more we remember Allah, the fewer mistakes we make!

Just like this:

	2	2	2
Sunday			
Monday			
Tuesday			
Wednesday			
Thursday			
Friday			
Saturday			

CHAPTER REVIEW

Healthy habit

Always remember that Shaytan is your enemy.
Always obey Allah and disobey Shaytan.

Study questions

1. What is the name of the first human Allah made? Was he a prophet?

2. Who disobeyed Allah when He told the angels to bow to Adam? What was his punishment?

3. What does Shaytan try to do to you?

4. What should you say if you do something bad? Why?

5. Whom should you remember always? Why?

6. What are the Names of Allah that mean "He forgives all of our mistakes?"

UNIT A CHAPTER 2

I Think of Allah First

questions?

1. Who is the One to think of before doing a good deed?
2. Who is the One we should try to please?
3. Who should be more important to us than playing, or eating, or sleeping?
4. How can we make sure we are doing the right thing?

word watch

niyyah	نيّة
Al-Awwal	الأوّل
Bismillah	بسم الله

Leena was so excited; she ran straight to her bedroom. Today she would get to open her new paint set! She had finished helping Mama and she had finished her homework, too! She was so happy!

Right when she sat down with some paper and paint, Leena heard the athan clock call for Maghrib prayer. She patiently waited for the athan to finish and said her du'aa. Then she started to paint.

Leena thought, "I think I can draw one picture before going to pray." As soon as Leena began painting, her mother came into the room.

Mama asked, "Leena, don't you think there is something more important that you should be doing?"

Leena answered sweetly, "I'm going to pray as soon as I finish this drawing, Mama!" Leena's mother shook her head and called Leena to come sit on the bed with her.

Mama asked, "Who gave you the paint set, Leena?"

Leena answered, "You and Baba did, Mama."

Mama asked, "And who gave you a Mama and a Baba?"

Leena answered, "Allah did!"

Mama said, "So don't you think you should thank Allah before you do anything else?"

Leena thought for a moment, "Without Allah, I would have nothing. I would have no paint set, no parents. I wouldn't even be here!"

Mama smiled, "That's right, my dear. And Allah created you and everyone else to worship Him."

Leena said, "I'm so glad you reminded me Who comes first, Mama! Let's go pray!"

We obey Allah FIRST because Allah is Special.

We obey Allah first. We should always remember Allah before anything and everything we do. One way we can do this is by doing every deed to make Allah happy. This way, we will always do good things.

WORDS OF WISDOM
HADEETH SHAREEF

حديث شريف
Narrated by Ahmed

عن أنس بن مالك رضي الله عنه: قال رسول الله ﷺ:

"لا يؤمن أحدكم حتى يكون الله ورسوله أحب إليه مما سِواهما" رواه أحمد

TRANSLITERATION

"La yo'minu ahadukum hatta yakoon Allah warasooluhu ahabba ilayhi mimma siwahuma."

TRANSLATION

Anas رضي الله عنه reported that Muhammad ﷺ said, "You will not be a true believer until you love God and His Messenger more than anything else."

Healthy
h a b i t

Before you begin anything, say:

بسم الله

Bismillah

This means: "In the Name of Allah"

A21

We should think of Allah first because it makes Him pleased with us. When we remember Allah before everything we do, He does nice things for us. Allah is a loving God. When we do things for God, we make it our **niyyah**, or intention, to please Him.

While Leena and her mother were praying Maghrib, Zaid and Baba were coming from the masjid. Zaid saw some empty cans lying in the grass. He ran to pick them up and threw them in the trash can.

Zaid said to his dad, "Allah made the world for us to live in, so we should take care of it! That's what Teacher Hibah taught me! I picked the trash up to keep our grass clean. I hope Allah will be happy with me." Zaid's father was very proud.

Zaid's father said, "Insha'Allah, Allah will give you many rewards (hasanat حسنات), Zaid. You had the right niyyah نِيَّة , because you picked up the trash to please and obey Allah.

Allah is Al-Awwal

الأوَّل

The First

Allah is the First, and we should always try to please Him first. Allah is the First because He was there before anything else.

CHAPTER REVIEW

Study questions

1. Who is the One we always try to please when doing any deed?

2. What should we say before doing any action?

3. What is the name of Allah in Arabic that means "The First?"

UNIT A CHAPTER 3

The Sons of Adam

questions?

1. Did Prophet Adam have children?
2. Did Prophet Adam's children obey Allah?
3. Do you know the names of Adam's children?

word watch

Habeel	هابيل
Qabeel	قابيل
Qayn	قَين
qurban	قُرْبان
Taqwa	تَقْوى

As you learned earlier, Allah sent Prophet Adam to live on Earth with his wife. They began a new family. They had **Habeel**, **Qabeel**, and some other children later. **Qayn** is another name for Qabeel.

When Habeel and Qabeel grew up, Allah ordered Habeel to marry one girl, and Qabeel to marry another. Habeel obeyed Allah, but Qabeel did not. He wanted to marry the girl that Allah had chosen for his brother. This was a problem! Both brothers could not marry the same girl!

Allah then told the two brothers to make a **qurban** (sacrifice) for Him. Qurban is something we give away for the sake of Allah. Habeel was a very good person. He loved Allah, and be always thought of Allah first. So he worked hard to offer Allah the best sacrifice he could find.

Qabeel was not as good as Habeel. He did not care much about pleasing Allah. He was selfish and thought of pleasing himself first. He brought a very small and cheap qurban. Allah accepted Habeel's sacrifice and rejected Qabeel's.

Qabeel became very jealous of his brother Habeel. Shaytan even made him think of killing Habeel so that he could marry the girl he liked. Qabeel told Habeel that he would kill him. Habeel was stronger than Qabeel, but he said, "If you do that, you will displease Allah, and you will lose. I will never kill you, because you are my brother."

A25

We should never get jealous of our Muslim brothers or sisters.

قال رسـول الله ﷺ :
"لا يؤمن أحدكم حتى يحب لأخيه ما يحب لنفسه"

The Prophet ﷺ said, "None of you truly believes until he loves for his brother what he loves for himself."

Remember, when we get angry or jealous, we become weak. It is easy for Shaytan to make us do bad things.

The first crime on Earth

Qabeel was on the wrong path. He listened to Shaytan and killed his brother! This was the first crime on Earth, and Qabeel was responsible for it.

Shaytan was leading Qabeel to Hell! He was a bad example for other people.

Healthy habit

Always be a good example so that others can learn good things from you.

Qabeel felt bad that he had killed his brother. He did not know what to do. He looked around and saw a bird burying a dead bird. Allah had sent the bird to teach Qabeel how to bury his brother.

Habeel was a hero. He was a good man, even though his brother was mean to him.

He had **taqwa** تقوى , and he pleased Allah. This means that he always obeyed Allah and feared His punishment. Habeel always tried to do the right thing.

CHAPTER REVIEW

ACTIVITY TIME

1. Act out a play with your friends about Habeel and Qabeel.

2. Write a short paragraph about what you would have done if you were in Qabeel's place.

Healthy habit

Always do good things to people. Always avoid hurting others.

Study questions

1. What were the names of Adam's sons?
2. Which son was good?
3. Which son was bad? How was he bad?
4. What made it easy for Shaytan to make Qabeel bad?
5. How should Muslims feel if something good happens to someone else?

UNIT A CHAPTER 4

My God Is My Creator

questions?

1. Can we pray to the sun, the moon, or statues?
2. Whom should we worship and pray to?
3. Why can we only worship and pray to Allah?

word watch

[إبراهيم   Ibraheem]

الله الخالق

Allah is the Creator

WORDS OF WISDOM
HOLY QUR'AN

سورة الأنعام
Surat Al-'An'am: ayah 162

بِسْمِ اللَّهِ الرَّحْمَٰنِ الرَّحِيمِ

قُلْ إِنَّ صَلَاتِي وَنُسُكِي وَمَحْيَايَ وَمَمَاتِي لِلَّهِ رَبِّ الْعَالَمِينَ

TRANSLITERATION

"Qul inna salati wa nusuki wa mahyaya wa mamati lillahi rabbil Alameen."

TRANSLATION

"Say indeed my prayer, my sacrifice, my living, and my dying are all for God, Lord of the Worlds."

Bilal: Dad, can you tell me a story?

Father: Okay, I know a good story about Prophet Ibraheem.

Ibraheem عليه السلام lived in Ur, a small town in Iraq. The people of Ur worshipped stones and statues.

A31

Ibraheem did not like that at all. He knew that these idols could not speak, hear, or see. They could not do any good or any harm. They could not feed the hungry or help the sick.

Ibraheem's father, Azar, was an idol maker. One day Ibraheem asked his father, "Why do you worship these stones that you have made, Father?"
Azar became angry and did not give a good answer.

One day, Ibraheem went to the idols when the people were away. He talked to them, but they could not talk back to him! So Ibraheem smashed one idol with his axe.

Of course, the other statues could not do anything. Then Ibraheem broke all the idols except the biggest one.

Ibraheem left the place. Later, the people came and saw all their idols broken. They were so angry!

They came to Ibraheem and asked, "Who has done this to our gods?"

"Ask the big one; he may know," answered Ibraheem.

The people knew that the idol could not answer them. They knew that Ibraheem had done it!

A34

They wanted to kill him.

The people were so angry that they wanted to kill Ibraheem!

They started a great fire and threw Ibraheem in it. They thought that Ibraheem would die, but he didn't.

Allah سبحانه وتعالى ordered the fire to be cool and safe for Ibraheem. Even the fire is obedient to Allah. It only burns when Allah commands it to burn. Allah saved Ibraheem, and he came out of the fire alive and safe.

Bilal: Allahu Akbar! I love Prophet Ibraheem عليه السلام ! He is my hero!

Healthy h a b i t

Always believe in Allah and put all your trust in Him.

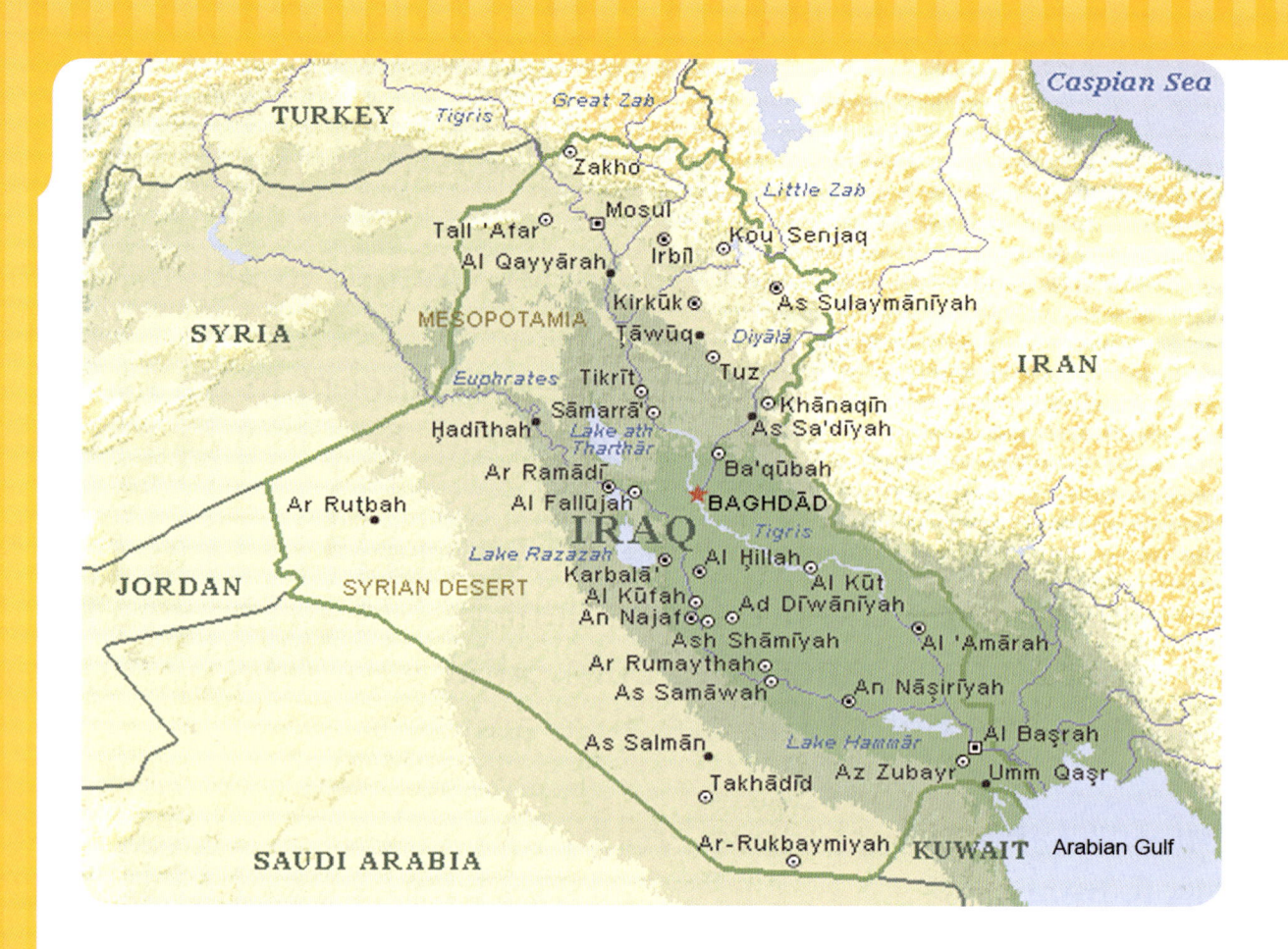

Iraq...

The Land Where Ibraheem Grew up

- Iraq is a Muslim land in Asia.
- It has two long rivers called the Tigris and the Euphrates.
- Iraq has about ninety million palm trees.
- The capital of Iraq is Baghdad.
- 25 million people live in Iraq, and most of them are Muslims.
- Iraq is a beautiful country.

CHAPTER REVIEW

ACTIVITY TIME

1. Open an atlas to the map of Iraq and try to draw it.

Study questions

1. Where was Prophet Ibraheem عليه السلام born?
2. What did his family worship?
3. What did Ibraheem do to the idols? Why?
4. What did the people do to Ibraheem?
5. How did Allah سبحانه وتعالى save Ibraheem?

UNIT A CHAPTER 5

I Trust Allah: The Story of Prophet Nuh

questions?

1. Whom do you trust the most?
2. What would you say if you saw someone building a ship far away from the sea?
3. What did Allah command Prophet Nuh to build? Why?
4. What did Prophet Nuh bring with him on the ark? How many of each?
5. Did people listen to Allah's command and go with Prophet Nuh on the ark?

word watch

[Nuh نُوْح
Judy جودي]

Many, many years passed after Prophet Adam left Jannah. Adam's children had children, and their children had children. The number of people on the Earth grew and grew. Soon, there were a lot of people all over the Earth!

More and more time passed, and people started to forget what Prophet Adam had taught. People all around the world found many ways to be bad - too many.

- People even forgot to worship the one true God!

- Some people prayed to idols that they made!

- Others killed their neighbors and relatives.

- Some ate and drank bad food, and even dead animals.

Allah was not happy with this. Allah knew that people on Earth needed a prophet to help them. Allah wanted His people to be good again. Allah chose **Nuh** to be the next prophet of Islam.

A39

Prophet Nuh did what Allah told him to do. He traveled from town to town talking to people. He told them to worship Allah alone. He also told them to stop doing bad things.

Prophet Nuh told the people that they could not worship idols. He warned them that if they did not stop their bad deeds, Allah would punish them.

Prophet Nuh taught his people to worship only their creator, Allah. He also taught them to do the right thing for 950 years, but only a few people listened! Most of them did not obey this great prophet. Allah finally told Prophet Nuh that bad people must be punished.

They were going to drown in a great flood.

The only people who would be safe were the people who believed in Allah and obeyed His prophet. Allah told Prophet Nuh to build an ark. An **ark** is a big boat.

People laughed at Prophet Nuh عليه السلام while he built his ark. They could not understand why he was building the ark. There was no ocean or river near their land. They also did not expect heavy rain to fall at that time. Prophet Nuh told them that they would not be laughing much longer.

Prophet Nuh took one pair of each living animal, a male and female. He put all of the animals on the ark, from the biggest elephant to the smallest ant. Allah helped him to do that.

One day, the people heard a scary noise in the sky. It was loud thunder. They also saw very bright lightning that got brighter and brighter. Seconds later, heavy rain started to fall. Springs began to rise up under people's feet.

Prophet Nuh عليه السلام and all the good people got on the ark. Prophet Nuh's wife and son Yam did not get on the ark! They did not obey Prophet Nuh. Nuh's son thought that he would be safe if he climbed on the highest mountain. Yam climbed, and he was sure that the water would not reach him there.

Prophet Nuh called his son: "Come on the ark, or you will drown." But his son did not believe in Allah and disobeyed his father. He stayed at the top of the mountain where he thought he would be safe. Prophet Nuh knew that his son would drown. Only the people on the ark would be safe. Allah had told Nuh the truth.

After many days and nights, Allah ordered the skies to stop their rain.

Allah commanded the Earth to swallow the water. The ark stopped floating and rested on a mountain called **Mount Judi**. Prophet Nuh and the believers were saved. All of the bad people were gone. Allah had kept His promise.

ACTIVITY TIME

1. Draw some of the animals that you think were on Prophet Nuh's ark.

WORDS OF WISDOM
HOLY QUR'AN

سورة القمر
Surat Al-Qamar: Ayaat 9-17

بِسْمِ ٱللَّهِ ٱلرَّحْمَٰنِ ٱلرَّحِيمِ

﴿ كَذَّبَتْ قَبْلَهُمْ قَوْمُ نُوحٍ فَكَذَّبُوا۟ عَبْدَنَا وَقَالُوا۟ مَجْنُونٌ وَٱزْدُجِرَ ۝٩ فَدَعَا رَبَّهُۥٓ أَنِّى مَغْلُوبٌ فَٱنتَصِرْ ۝١٠ فَفَتَحْنَآ أَبْوَٰبَ ٱلسَّمَآءِ بِمَآءٍ مُّنْهَمِرٍ ۝١١ وَفَجَّرْنَا ٱلْأَرْضَ عُيُونًا فَٱلْتَقَى ٱلْمَآءُ عَلَىٰٓ أَمْرٍ قَدْ قُدِرَ ۝١٢ وَحَمَلْنَٰهُ عَلَىٰ ذَاتِ أَلْوَٰحٍ وَدُسُرٍ ۝١٣ تَجْرِى بِأَعْيُنِنَا جَزَآءً لِّمَن كَانَ كُفِرَ ۝١٤ وَلَقَد تَّرَكْنَٰهَآ ءَايَةً فَهَلْ مِن مُّدَّكِرٍ ۝١٥ فَكَيْفَ كَانَ عَذَابِى وَنُذُرِ ۝١٦ وَلَقَدْ يَسَّرْنَا ٱلْقُرْءَانَ لِلذِّكْرِ فَهَلْ مِن مُّدَّكِرٍ ۝١٧ ﴾

TRANSLITERATION

[9] Kaththabat qablahum qawmu nuhin fakhaththaboo 'abdana waqaloo majnoonuw-wazdujir

[10] Fada'a rabbahu annee maghloobun fantasir

[11] Fafatahna abwab-as-sama'i bima'im munhamir

[12] Wafajjarnal-'arda 'uyoonan faltaqal-ma'o 'ala 'amrin qad qudir

[13] Wahamalnahu 'ala thati alwahiw wadusur

[14] Tajree bi-a'ayunina jaza'al liman kana kufir

[15] Walaqad taraknaha 'ayatan fahal mim-muddakir

[16] Fakayfa kana 'athabee wanuthur

[17] Walaqad yassarnal qur'ana liththikri fahal mim muddakir

TRANSLATION

[9] Before them the People of Noah rejected (their messenger): they rejected Our servant, and said, "Here is one possessed!" and he was driven out.

[10] Then he called on his Lord: "I am overcome: then help (me)!"

[11] So We opened the gates of heaven, with water pouring forth.

[12] And We caused the Earth to gush forth with springs, so the waters met (and rose) up.

[13] But We bore him on an (Ark) made of broad planks and caulked with palm-fibre:

[14] She floats under our eyes (and care): a reward to one who had been rejected!

[15] And We have left this as a Sign (for all time): then is there any that will receive admonition?

[16] But how (terrible) was My Penalty and My Warning?

[17] And We have indeed made the Qur'an easy to understand and remember: then is there any one that will remember?

CHAPTER REVIEW

Study questions

1. Who was Nuh?
2. What did Allah command him to do? Why?
3. How did the Earth change at that time?
4. Who obeyed Prophet Nuh? Who did not obey him? What happened to those who obeyed? What happened to those who disobeyed?

UNIT A CHAPTER 6

Turning to Allah: The Story Of Prophet Younus

questions?

1. What would you do if you were trapped in a small, dark place?
2. Whom should you always turn to if you need something?
3. Why did Allah send prophets to His people?

word watch

Younus ibn Matta	يونس ابن مطة
Naynawa	نِينَوى
sabr	صَبر
Du'aa	دُعاء
tasbeeh	تَسبيحْ
As-Samee	السَّميع

Allah سبحانه وتعالى loves His servants very much. Allah sent many prophets to show people the right way to Jannah.

One of Allah's prophets was a man called **Younus ibn Matta** يونس ابن مطة.

A48

Allah سبحانه وتعالى chose Younus from among the people to be their prophet.
Younus and his people lived in a village called **Naynawa** in Iraq.

Younus عليه السلام started teaching his people Islam. He called upon them to worship only one God, Allah. They did not want to obey him.

Prophet Younus عليه السلام was afraid for his people because they did not believe in Allah سبحانه وتعالى. He warned them that if they didn't believe in Allah, they would be punished after three days.

They laughed at Prophet Younus and did not obey him.

Prophet Younus عليه السلام became angry, and he decided to leave the village of Naynawa. He left the village without getting permission from Allah. Younus got aboard a ship and sailed away from his people.

While Younus عليه السلام was on the ship, A STRONG STORM CAME.

The ship was about to sink!

People on board started throwing their belongings into the water. They wanted to keep the boat above the water.

The ship was still going to sink.

They thought that the boat would sink because too many people were on it. So, they decided to throw at least one person in the water. They drew names many times, and the name of Younus came up each time! Younus was thrown into the sea.

ALONG CAME A BIG WHALE!

When Prophet Younus عليه السلام was in the water, a big whale came and swallowed him. Allah سبحانه وتعالى ordered the whale not to hurt Younus while he was in his stomach.

Now, Prophet Younus was in the stomach of the whale. It was so dark and wet.

Younus was in three types of darkness:

1. He was inside the stomach of the whale
2. He was deep under water.
3. It was nighttime.

> It must have been
> # SO SCARY
> for Prophet Younus!

Younus عليه السلام realized that he had left his people without waiting for permission from Allah سبحانه وتعالى. He knew he should have been more patient with his people. He started asking Allah for forgiveness and saying that he had been wrong.

THE POWER OF
Du'aa and Tasbeeh

﴿ فَنَادَىٰ فِي ٱلظُّلُمَٰتِ أَن لَّآ إِلَٰهَ إِلَّآ أَنتَ سُبْحَٰنَكَ إِنِّى كُنتُ مِنَ ٱلظَّٰلِمِينَ ﴾

I have been wrong.

"And he called out within the darknesses, 'There is no God except You; exalted are You. Indeed, I have been of the wrongdoers.'" Surat Al-'Anbya' ayah 87

That was the **du'aa** and **tasbeeh** of Prophet Younus during his days and nights in the whale's stomach. He said it over and over again.

Healthy habit

Always be patient if something bad happens, and always ask Allah for forgiveness if you become angry.

Healthy habit

When you are upset, sad, and need Allah's help, say:

"لا إله إلا أنت سبحانك إنّي كُنت من الظالمين."

"La ilaha illa anta subhanaka innee kuntu mina-thalimeen."

This means: "There is no God except You; exalted are You. Indeed, I have been of the wrongdoers."

> This time, Prophet Younus learned his lesson and showed **sabr**. This means that he was patient and waited for Allah to do what was best.

Allah heard Prophet Younus's du'aa.

Allah is As-Samee'

السّميع

All-Hearing

A55

Allah سبحانه وتعالى made the whale come on shore and spit Younus out of his stomach. Prophet Younus عليه السلام was very sick when he came out.

Allah allowed a gourd tree with big leaves to grow over Younus. Now he could eat from its fruit. Younus rested under its big leaves until he became well enough to go back to his people in Naynawa. He began his journey home.

Meanwhile, in the village of Naynawa, a strong and powerful wind started to blow. The people were scared. Now, they knew that Younus was a prophet from Allah. They were sorry that they had not obeyed Younus, and they began to worship only Allah. Now, all of the people of Naynawa became believers.

They started praying and making du'aa to Allah to stop His punishment and to forgive them.

> Allah سبحانه وتعالى is so merciful and forgiving, that He answered their du'aa. Allah forgave them and stopped the storm.

WORDS OF WISDOM
HOLY QUR'AN

سورة الصافات
Surat As-Saffat: ayaat 139-148

بِسْمِ اللَّهِ الرَّحْمَٰنِ الرَّحِيمِ

وَإِنَّ يُونُسَ لَمِنَ الْمُرْسَلِينَ ﴿١٣٩﴾ إِذْ أَبَقَ إِلَى الْفُلْكِ الْمَشْحُونِ ﴿١٤٠﴾ فَسَاهَمَ فَكَانَ مِنَ الْمُدْحَضِينَ ﴿١٤١﴾ فَالْتَقَمَهُ الْحُوتُ وَهُوَ مُلِيمٌ ﴿١٤٢﴾ فَلَوْلَا أَنَّهُ كَانَ مِنَ الْمُسَبِّحِينَ ﴿١٤٣﴾ لَلَبِثَ فِي بَطْنِهِ إِلَىٰ يَوْمِ يُبْعَثُونَ ﴿١٤٤﴾ ۞ فَنَبَذْنَاهُ بِالْعَرَاءِ وَهُوَ سَقِيمٌ ﴿١٤٥﴾ وَأَنبَتْنَا عَلَيْهِ شَجَرَةً مِّن يَقْطِينٍ ﴿١٤٦﴾ وَأَرْسَلْنَاهُ إِلَىٰ مِائَةِ أَلْفٍ أَوْ يَزِيدُونَ ﴿١٤٧﴾ فَآمَنُوا فَمَتَّعْنَاهُمْ إِلَىٰ حِينٍ ﴿١٤٨﴾

TRANSLITERATION

[139] Wa-inna younusa lamin almursaleen
[140] Ith abaqa ilal-fulk-il-mash-hoon
[141] Fasahama fakana min-al-mud-hadeen
[142] Faltaqamah-ul-hootu wahuwa muleem
[143] Falawla annahu kana min-al-musabbiheen
[144] Lalabitha fee batnihi ila yawmi yub'athoon
[145] Fanabathnahu bil'ara-i wahuwa saqeem
[146] Wa-anbatna 'alayhi shajaratam-miy-yaqteen
[147] Wa'arsalnahu ila mi'ati alfin aw yazeedoon
[148] Fa'amanoo famatta'nahum ila heen

TRANSLATION

[139] ...And Younus was among the messengers,

[140] when he ran away without permission to the ship that was full.

[141] He made a draw and lost [thus he was thrown overboard].

[142] Then the whale swallowed him, which he deserved.

[143] And if he had not been among those who praised [Allah],

[144] He would have remained inside the whale till the Day of Judgment.

[145] But We cast him away on the open shore, and he was sick.

[146] And We shaded him with a gourd tree,

[147] And We sent him [as a messenger] to a hundred thousand (people) or more.

[148] And they believed; so We made them enjoy (their life) for a while.

Healthy habit

Always make du'aa to Allah to help you. Ask Him for help before you ask anybody else. Make du'aa every day, and every time you need help, even if it is for a small thing.

Do you know how many people lived in the town of Naynawa?

More than 100,000 people!

That means there were 100,000 more believers!

This means Allah answers du'aa and prayers.

When Younus felt better, he returned to Naynawa. To his surprise, all of the people welcomed him! He was so happy.
He started teaching them Islam, and this time, they listened to him.

CHAPTER REVIEW

ACTIVITY TIME

1. Draw a whale swimming in the sea under a ship.

2. Write a short paragraph about what you would do if you were in the stomach of the whale.

Study questions

1. What did Prophet Younus try to teach his people? At first, did they listen?

2. What did Prophet Younus do when his people disobeyed him? Was this the right thing to do?

3. What happened to Younus in the sea?

4. When Younus realized his mistake, what did he do?

5. How did Allah show Younus that He had forgiven him?

6. When you make a mistake, and need help from Allah. What should you do and say?

UNIT A CHAPTER 7

Taqwa: Allah Sees Me All the Time

questions?

1. If you are alone in your room, is there anyone who can see you?
2. Who can see and hear you all the time?

word watch

taqwa	تَقْوى
Al-Aleem	العَليم
Al-Khabeer	الخَبير
Al-Baseer	البَصير

In Al-Qur'an, Allah said that Luqman the wise man told his son:

"O my son, indeed if it would be the weight of a mustard seed and should be in a rock or anywhere in the Heavens or on the Earth, Allah will bring it forth. Indeed Allah is knowledgable." Surat Luqman: ayah 16

Allah knows where everything is. Just like this ayah says, if a small, tiny seed is inside a rock, on the Earth, or in the Heavens, Allah knows about it.

Allah can see a tiny ant moving fast on a black rock.

think about it!

When you are by yourself with no one around, do you think you are alone?

When you see two or three people talking, do you think they are alone?

If you answered "NO," you are "CORRECT."

When a person is by himself, Allah is watching him.
When two people are talking, Allah is watching them. He is the third.
When three people are talking, Allah is watching them. He is the fourth.
When you whisper to your friend and you think no one else can hear you, Allah can.
Allah says:

﴿ إِنَّ ٱللَّهَ بِكُلِّ شَيْءٍ عَلِيمٌ ﴾

"Allah has full knowledge of all things." Surat Al-Mujadila:7

Allah knows what you are going to say before you say it. Allah knows what you do even when you think no one can see you.

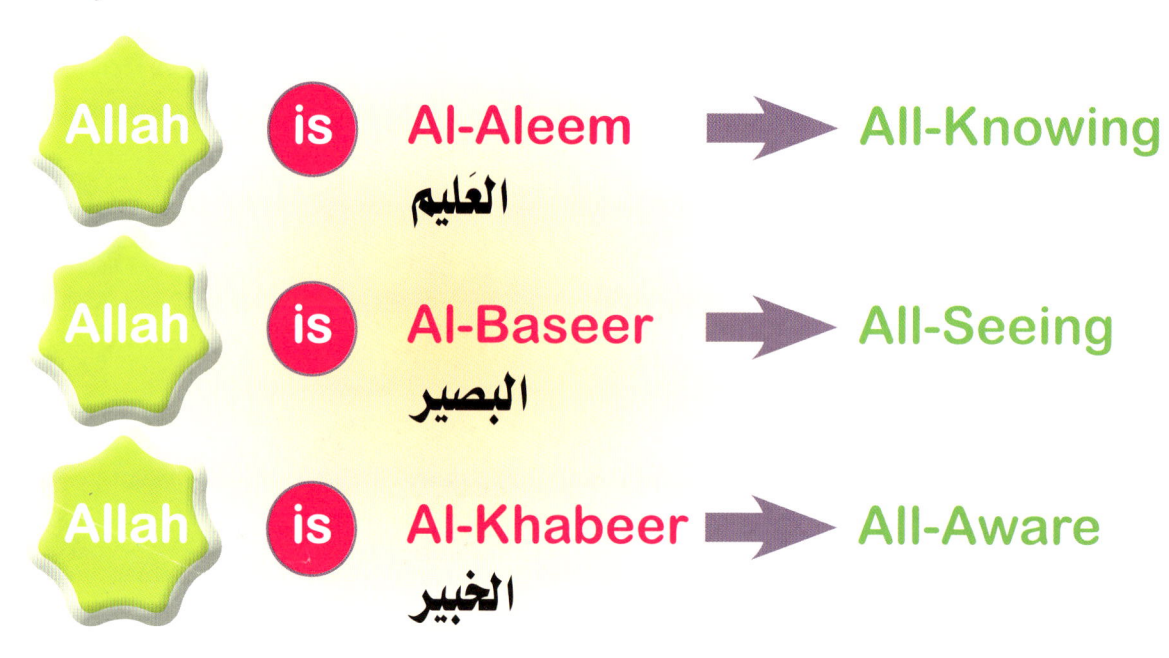

Allah	is	Al-Aleem العَليم	➡	All-Knowing
Allah	is	Al-Baseer البصير	➡	All-Seeing
Allah	is	Al-Khabeer الخبير	➡	All-Aware

Taqwa is Great

Khalid and Amir were good friends. They were walking home from school one day. They were passing through a garden when they saw a big apple tree. There were so many fresh apples hanging from the tree!

Without thinking, Amir started climbing on the tree to pick some apples. He asked his friend Khalid to watch for anyone around. As soon as Amir started climbing, Khalid yelled, "Come down, Amir. Somebody can see you!" Amir replied, "Where? I don't see anyone." Then Amir climbed the tree again. Khalid yelled again, "Somebody can see you!" When Amir finally came down, he asked Khalid, "What do you mean somebody can see me? I don't see anyone. Do you?"

Khalid was being a good friend. He reminded Amir by saying, "Someone can see you. Allah سبحانه وتعالى can see you. And we should do the right thing, whether we are alone or with others."

This is taqwa

Amir nodded his head and regretted what he did. He realized that he should not have taken something that did not belong to him.

Amir looked at his friend and said, "Jazak Allahu khayran, Khalid." Khalid smiled and said, "That's what friends are for." As the two friends were leaving the garden, the owner came out and yelled, "Would you like to have some apples, boys?"

Khalid said: "Subhan'Allah, taqwa is good. It gives you good rewards, and apples, too!"

WORDS OF WISDOM

HOLY QUR'AN

سورة التوبة

Surat At-Tawbah: ayah 4

إِنَّ ٱللَّهَ يُحِبُّ ٱلْمُتَّقِينَ

TRANSLITERATION

InnAllaha yuhibb-ul-muttaqeen

TRANSLATION

Indeed, God loves the righteous.

Nowhere to Hide

Let us read another story together:

One day, Zaid's grandfather was visiting Zaid's family. Bilal was at Zaid's home, too. Grandfather called all the children. He wanted to teach the children a lesson about the power of Allah سبحانه وتعالى . All the children hurried to him: Zaid, Leena, and Bilal.

Grandfather gave each one of them a cupcake that their grandmother had made. The grandfather asked the children to eat the cupcakes in a place where no one could see them. "Each one of you find a place where no one can see you, and eat your cupcake there," Grandfather said. Leena went inside her room, said "Bismillah," and ate her cupcake.

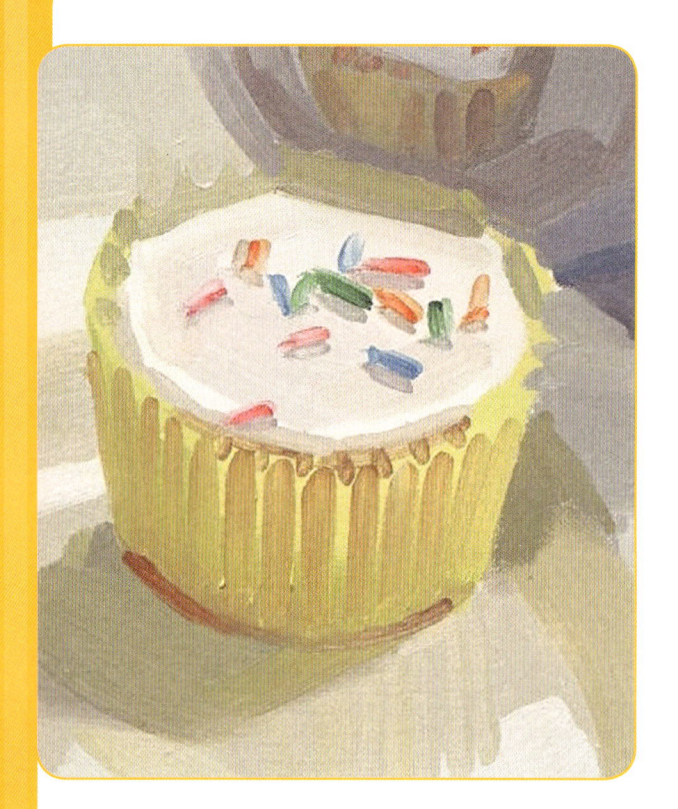

Bilal went out to the garden and climbed up to the tree house where he was by himself. He said "Bismillah," and ate his cupcake.

At the same time, Zaid was still looking for a place to be alone.

Finally, he went back to his grandfather and said, "Grandfather, everywhere I went, I was not alone. I knew Allah سبحانه وتعالى was watching over me and protecting me. So I am never alone."

Grandfather Mahmoud called Leena and Bilal and told them what Zaid said.

The three children learned an important lesson.

No matter where we go, Allah is always with us, watching us, and protecting us.

﴿ إِنَّ ٱللَّهَ لَا يَخْفَىٰ عَلَيْهِ شَيْءٌ فِى ٱلْأَرْضِ وَلَا فِى ٱلسَّمَآءِ ﴾

"Indeed, from Allah nothing is hidden: on the Earth nor in Heaven."
Al-'Imran: ayah 5

> We should always do what is right, because Allah knows all secrets.

What is Taqwa?

Once somebody asked Omar ibn-ul-Khattab: What is taqwa?

He said: Did you ever walk through a land with many thorny bushes?

The Man answered: Yes.
Omar: What did you do?

Man: I tried my best not to touch the thorns, so they would not poke me.

Omar: This is **taqwa**. You try your best not to sin, because sins displease Allah and hurt you.

WORDS OF WISDOM
HOLY QUR'AN

سورة البلد
Surat Al-Balad

بِسْمِ ٱللَّهِ ٱلرَّحْمَٰنِ ٱلرَّحِيمِ

لَا أُقْسِمُ بِهَٰذَا ٱلْبَلَدِ ۝١ وَأَنتَ حِلٌّ بِهَٰذَا ٱلْبَلَدِ ۝٢ وَوَالِدٍ وَمَا وَلَدَ ۝٣ لَقَدْ خَلَقْنَا ٱلْإِنسَٰنَ فِى كَبَدٍ ۝٤ أَيَحْسَبُ أَن لَّن يَقْدِرَ عَلَيْهِ أَحَدٌ ۝٥ يَقُولُ أَهْلَكْتُ مَالًا لُّبَدًا ۝٦ أَيَحْسَبُ أَن لَّمْ يَرَهُۥٓ أَحَدٌ ۝٧ أَلَمْ نَجْعَل لَّهُۥ عَيْنَيْنِ ۝٨ وَلِسَانًا وَشَفَتَيْنِ ۝٩ وَهَدَيْنَٰهُ ٱلنَّجْدَيْنِ ۝١٠ فَلَا ٱقْتَحَمَ ٱلْعَقَبَةَ ۝١١ وَمَآ أَدْرَىٰكَ مَا ٱلْعَقَبَةُ ۝١٢ فَكُّ رَقَبَةٍ ۝١٣ أَوْ إِطْعَٰمٌ فِى يَوْمٍ ذِى مَسْغَبَةٍ ۝١٤ يَتِيمًا ذَا مَقْرَبَةٍ ۝١٥ أَوْ مِسْكِينًا ذَا مَتْرَبَةٍ ۝١٦ ثُمَّ كَانَ مِنَ ٱلَّذِينَ ءَامَنُوا۟ وَتَوَاصَوْا۟ بِٱلصَّبْرِ وَتَوَاصَوْا۟ بِٱلْمَرْحَمَةِ ۝١٧ أُو۟لَٰٓئِكَ أَصْحَٰبُ ٱلْمَيْمَنَةِ ۝١٨ وَٱلَّذِينَ كَفَرُوا۟ بِـَٔايَٰتِنَا هُمْ أَصْحَٰبُ ٱلْمَشْـَٔمَةِ ۝١٩ عَلَيْهِمْ نَارٌ مُّؤْصَدَةٌۢ ۝٢٠

TRANSLITERATION

[1] La 'oqsimu bihathal-balad
[2] Wa'anta hillum bihathal-balad
[3] Wawalidiw wama walad
[4] Laqad khalaqnal-insana fee kabad
[5] Ayahsabu al-lay-yaqdira 'alayhi ahad
[6] Yaqoolu ahlaktu malal-lubada
[7] Ayahsabu al-lam yarahu ahad
[8] Alam naj'al lahu 'aynayn
[9] Walisanaw-washafatayn
[10] Wahadaynah-un-najdayn
[11] Falaqtaham-al'aqabah
[12] Wama 'adraka mal-'aqabah
[13] Fakku raqabah
[14] Aw it'amun fee yawmin thee masghabah
[15] Yateeman tha maqrabah
[16] Aw miskeenan tha matrabah
[17] Thumma kana min-allatheena amanoo watawasaw bissabri watawasaw bilmarhamah
[18] Olaa'ika as-hab-ul-maymanah
[19] Waallatheena kafaroo bi'aayatina hum as-hab-ul-mash'amah
[20] 'alayhim narum mu'sadah

TRANSLATION

[1] By this city [Makkah];
[2] And you are free men in this city;
[3] And by a parent and his child;
[4] We have created man into a struggle.
[5] Does he think that no one has power over him?
[6] He may say: "I have spent a lot of money!"
[7] Does he think that no one watches over him?
[8] Have We not made for him two eyes?
[9] And a tongue, and two lips?
[10] And shown him the two ways [good and evil]?
[11] But he has made no haste on the path that is steep.
[12] And what do you know about the path that is steep?
[13] (It is:) freeing the slave;
[14] Or giving food in a day of hunger
[15] To the orphan that is a relative,
[16] Or to the poor in the dust.
[17] Then will he be of those who believe, and call for patience and kindness.
[18] Those are the people of the right hand [They will receive their books of deeds by their right hands].
[19] But those who reject Our signs, they are the (unhappy) people of the left hand [They will receive their books of deeds by their left hands].
[20] On them the Fire will be raised (all round).

A Poem

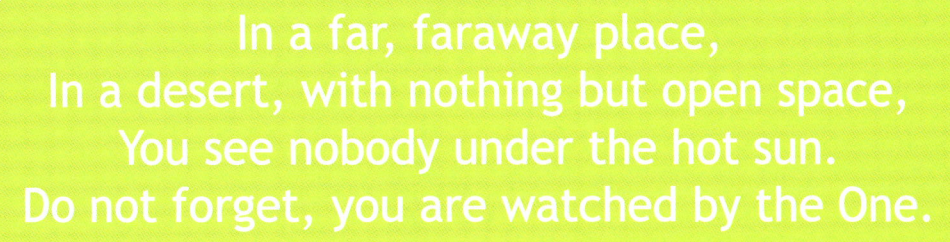

In a far, faraway place,
In a desert, with nothing but open space,
You see nobody under the hot sun.
Do not forget, you are watched by the One.

ALLAH!

CHAPTER REVIEW

Study questions

1. What is taqwa?

2. Why is taqwa good for you?

3. Who sees and hears you all the time?

4. Why did Khalid tell Amir not to pick apples from the tree in the garden? What happened when they were leaving?

5. What did Zaid's grandfather tell the children to do? Why?

6. What happened at the end?

7. Write three lessons you have learned from the stories in this chapter.

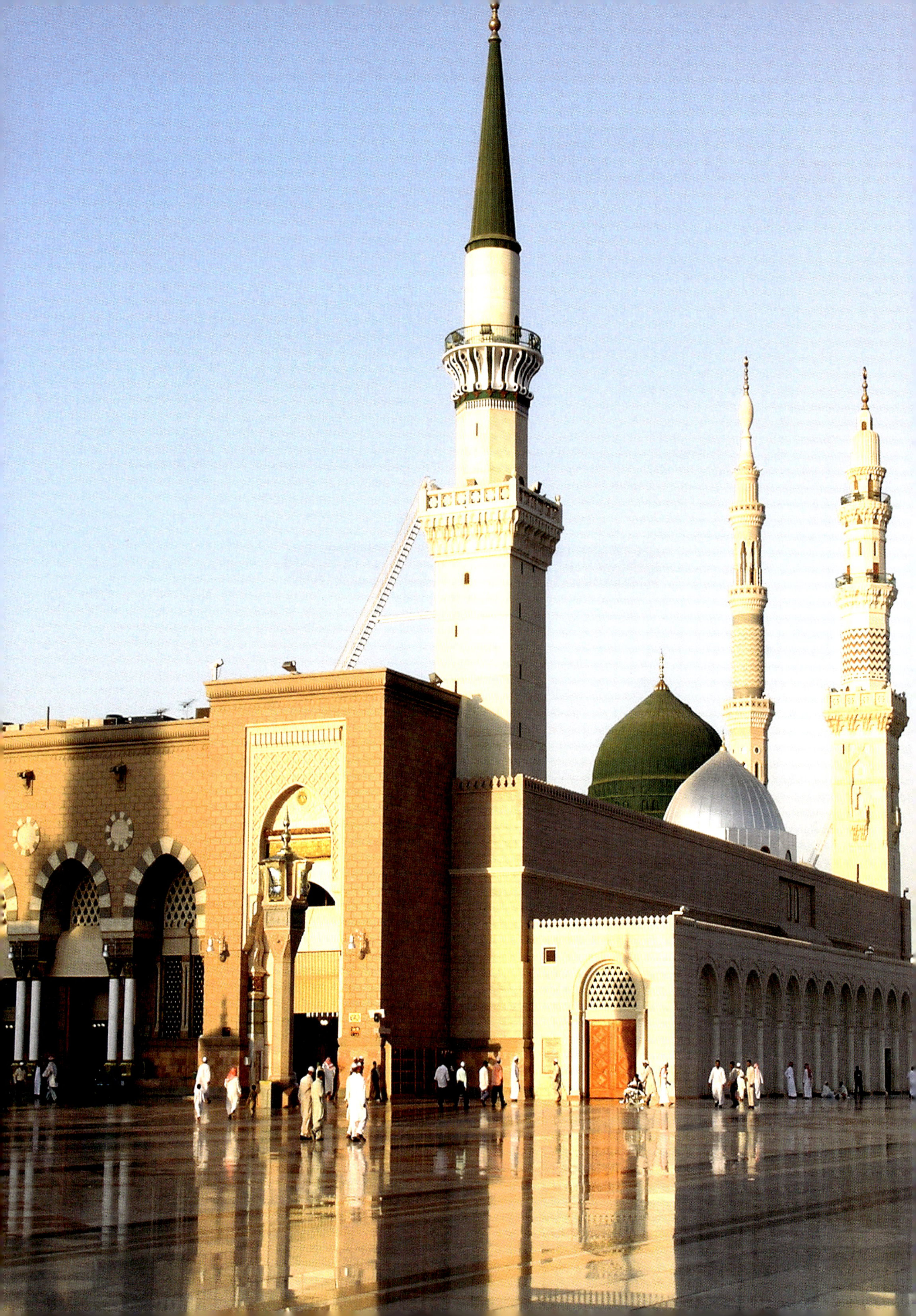

UNIT B

I LOVE MUHAMMAD ﷺ

Chapter 1	Aam-ul-Feel: The Year of the Elephant ... B2
Chapter 2	Muhammad: The Praised Child B12
Chapter 3	The Orphan B22
Chapter 4	The Blessed Young Man B34
Chapter 5	As-Sadiq Al-Ameen: The Truthful, the Trusted B42
Chapter 6	The Happy Marriage B52
Chapter 7	Zaid Bin Harithah B58
Chapter 8	Prophet Muhammad Loves Children B68

UNIT B CHAPTER 1
Amm-ul-Feel: The Year of the Elephant

questions?

1. What does the Arabic word "feel" mean in English?
2. Where is Al-Ka'bah?

word watch

iman	إيمان
Makkah	مكة
Al-Ka'bah	الكعبة
Abdul-Muttalib	عبد المطلب
Abraha	أبرهة

Yemen is a country that is south of old Arabia, or Saudi Arabia now.

A long time ago, the ruler of Yemen was a bad man named Abraha.

ACTIVITY TIME

Point to Makkah and Yemen on the map of Saudi Arabia.

The holy Ka'bah is in Makkah, in Arabia. **Makkah** is a very special place. It was built by Prophets Ibraheem and Isma'eel a very long time ago. Allah told them to build it. **Al-Ka'bah** was the first house of worship built on Earth. People in Arabia honored Al-Ka'bah and visited Makkah very often.

Abraha was very jealous that the people loved Al-Ka'bah and Makkah so much. People did not come to visit his own country, Yemen. He decided to build a big church in Yemen for everybody to visit.

Abraha wanted people to love his church as much as Al-Ka'bah, or even more. He even asked people to stop visiting Al-Ka'bah and come to his church instead. The Arabs did not listen, and they kept on visiting Al-Ka'bah. This made Abraha very mad. Some Arabs were in Abraha's church one day and ruined a part of it. This made Abraha very angry. He decided to destroy Al-Ka'bah once and for all!

Abraha gathered a HUGE army and went to Makkah. He also took some HUGE elephants to help him destroy Al-Ka'bah.

He stopped just outside of Makkah and sent some of his soldiers to see what was around. On their way, they captured the camels and herds belonging to the people of Makkah. This would make it hard for the people of Makkah to fight Abraha. Many of the camels belonged to **Abdul-Muttalib**, the leader of Makkah.

Abdul-Muttalib went with some of his sons to see Abraha. Abraha thought that Abdul-Muttalib was going to ask him not to destroy Al-Ka'bah. Instead he asked Abraha to return his camels. Abraha asked Abdul-Muttalib why he was worrying about his camels and not about Al-Ka'bah.

Abdul-Mutallib told Abraha:
"I am the owner of the camels, so I protect them, while Al-Ka'bah has a Lord who will protect it."

Abdul Muttalib meant that Allah would look after Al-Ka'bah.

Abraha did not believe this, and he shook his head and said:
"No one can stop me from destroying Al-Ka'bah!"

Abdul-Muttalib had **iman**, or faith, that Allah would protect Al-Ka'bah. He ordered the people to leave Makkah and go to the hills for safety. He then prayed to Allah to protect them and Al-Ka'bah from any harm.

The next morning, Abraha marched to Al-Ka'bah. He wanted to attack it with all of his elephants. Abraha had trained the lead elephant to obey orders like. . .

Sit! Go Forward!
Turn around!

Abraha ordered the elephants to destroy Al-Ka'bah, but whenever they were told to go to Al-Ka'bah, they would run away from it. The elephants refused to destroy Al-Ka'bah because they were obeying the commands of Allah, not Abraha!

Then all of a sudden, a flock of birds appeared in the sky. They were holding stones in their claws and beaks.

By the command of Allah, each bird dropped the stones onto Abraha and his army, causing a shower of stones.

These stones hit Abraha and his army, hurting them very badly. Abraha and his army were all destroyed. Allah stopped Abraha from destroying Al-Ka'bah. Abdul-Muttalib had trusted Allah, and his prayer was answered.

ACTIVITY TIME

Make a model of Al-Ka'bah

Allah saved His house, Al-Ka'bah.

He destroyed Abraha and his army.

WORDS OF WISDOM
HOLY QUR'AN

سورة الفيل
Surat Al-Feel

بِسْمِ اللَّهِ الرَّحْمَٰنِ الرَّحِيمِ

أَلَمْ تَرَ كَيْفَ فَعَلَ رَبُّكَ بِأَصْحَابِ الْفِيلِ ۝ أَلَمْ يَجْعَلْ كَيْدَهُمْ فِي تَضْلِيلٍ ۝ وَأَرْسَلَ عَلَيْهِمْ طَيْرًا أَبَابِيلَ ۝ تَرْمِيهِم بِحِجَارَةٍ مِّن سِجِّيلٍ ۝ فَجَعَلَهُمْ كَعَصْفٍ مَّأْكُولٍ ۝

TRANSLITERATION

[1] Alam tara kayfa fa'ala rabbuka bi'as-hab-il-feal
[2] Alam yaj'al kaydahum fee tadleel
[3] Wa'arsala 'alayhim tayran ababeel
[4] Tarmeehim bihijaratin min sijjeel
[5] Faja'alahum ka'asfim-ma'kool

TRANSLATION

[1] Didn't you know how your Lord dealt with the people of the elephant?
[2] Didn't He ruin their evil plan?
[3] And He sent against them birds in flocks,
[4] Striking them with stones of hard clay,
[5] And He made them like eaten straw.

CHAPTER REVIEW

ACTIVITY TIME

1. Draw an elephant near Al-Ka'bah.

2. Make a play about Abdul-Muttalib and Abraha.

Study questions

1. Why did Abraha want to destroy Al-Ka'bah?

2. Who is Abdul-Muttalib? What made him tell the people of Makkah to leave?

3. Why was Abdul-Muttalib not worried about Al-Ka'bah?

4. What happened when Abraha told the elephant to destroy Al-Ka'bah?

5. How did Allah protect Al-Ka'bah?

UNIT B CHAPTER 2
Muhammad ﷺ: The Praised Child

questions?

1. When was Prophet Muhammad ﷺ born?
2. Who were the parents of Prophet Muhammad ﷺ?
3. Where was the Prophet ﷺ sent as a young baby, and why?
4. Who took care of him there?

word watch

Yathrib	يثرب
Seerah	سيرة
Aminah	أمينة
Haleemah	حليمة

One day, in Zaid's Islamic studies class, Teacher Hibah began telling a story. Zaid listened very carefully. It was a story about a great young boy who went through very sad times. It sounded like a very interesting and special story.

Teacher Hibah: Class, do you remember when we talked about the Year of the Elephant and Al-Ka'bah?

Class: Yes, we do, Teacher Hibah!

Teacher Hibah: The Year of the Elephant was the beginning of the life of someone we all love so much. His life is a very special story. It is called **Seerah**: the story of the life of Prophet MUHAMMAD ﷺ !

Healthy habit

Always listen carefully to what your teachers and elders tell you.

Teacher Hibah began the story:

Abdullah Marries Aminah

In the Year of the Elephant, there were two wonderful families living in Makkah. One was the Abdul-Muttalib family, and the other was the Wahb family. Abdullah was the youngest son of Abdul-Muttalib, and the most loved. **Aminah** was the daughter of Wahb, who was a kind man in Makkah. Aminah was a great and sweet young lady. Abdullah wanted Aminah to be his wife because she and her family were so good and kind. Aminah and Abdullah got married that year.

Abdullah Dies

A few months later, Abdul-Muttalib sent his son Abdullah to buy some dates from **Yathrib**, a small town not very far north of Makkah. On his way back, Abdullah became very sick. Soon after that, Abdullah died. Aminah became very sad and missed her husband very much.

Muhammad is Born!

One night, Aminah dreamt that a great light came out of her and lightened up all of Arabia! She also dreamt that a sweet voice was telling her, "You are bearing a great boy. When he is born, name him Muhammad." A few months later, our beloved Prophet Muhammad ﷺ was born!

Teacher Hibah: As you see, Prophet Muhammad's ﷺ father died before he was born. Isn't that so sad for Aminah and Baby Muhammad ﷺ? We should be thankful to Allah that we have our parents!

Healthy habit

1. Always thank Allah for giving you caring parents.

2. Obey your parents and always be kind and nice to them.

Baby Muhammad with Haleemah

When Prophet Muhammad ﷺ was a few months old, his family sent him to the desert to live with a nice lady named **Haleemah**.

Zaid: Why was he sent to the desert away from his family?

Teacher Hibah: Good question, Zaid. Babies of noble families in Makkah were sent to live their first years in the desert. There, they could breathe the clean and pure air, eat healthy food, and grow strong. Also, people who lived in the desert spoke beautiful Arabic, so these babies learned to speak good Arabic as they grew up.

Muhammad ﷺ brought Haleemah's family many blessings. Haleemah took good care of him. She taught him to be a nice boy. Muhammad always kept himself nice and clean. Muhammad ﷺ was loved very much by Haleemah and her family. He also had many friends because he was so friendly and kind.

Teacher Hibah: See how nicely the Prophet ﷺ acted, even when he was a small child? Allah was showing us how we should act, no matter how old we are.

Mona: I love Prophet Muhammad ﷺ, and I will try to be as nice as he was!

Class: We will, too!

Nasheed

Ya Muhammad

Praise him throughout the land.
Allah sent him here to guide us with
the Message of Islam.

In the town of Makkah, long ago,
a baby boy was born.
Near the Ka'bah, Allah's holy house,
upon a Monday morn.
With hair of black and eyes of brown,
a lovely child was he!
With a smile so sweet that all agreed
a special man he'd be.

Though mother, father, he had
none, an orphan it is true.
He always did his very best to give
the poor their due.
He was kind to every man and beast,
to rich and poor alike.
He was fair because he saw them all
as equal in God's sight.

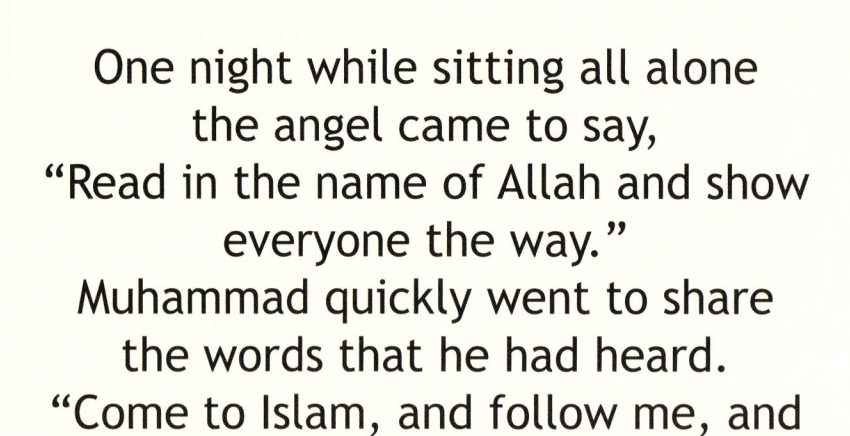

One night while sitting all alone
the angel came to say,
"Read in the name of Allah and show
everyone the way."
Muhammad quickly went to share
the words that he had heard.
"Come to Islam, and follow me, and
heed God's Holy Word."

For years and years Muhammad
worked and never took a rest.
So that you and I would be Muslims and
pass Allah's great test.
With patience, kindness, care and love
Muhammad gathered all
To worship Allah, Lord above,
and now we loudly call!

Allah sent him here to guide us
with His Holy book Qur'an.
Allah sent him here to guide us
with the Message of Islam.
Ya Muhmmad! Praise his Name!

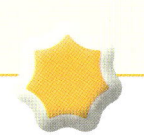

Listen to this nasheed on Track 4 of your CD.

CHAPTER REVIEW

Healthy habit

Always be nice and kind with your friends, so they will be nice and kind with you. Treat them like your brothers and sisters.

Study questions

1. What is the Seerah about?

2. Who was the father of Prophet Muhammad ﷺ? Who was his mother?

3. How did Allah let Aminah know that someone special would be coming into her life?

4. Why was the Prophet ﷺ sent to the desert as a small child?

5. What was the name of the kind woman who took care of Muhammad ﷺ in the desert?

6. Why was she so happy with Muhammad ﷺ?

UNIT B CHAPTER 3

The Orphan

questions?

1. How did Allah reward Haleemah's family for their kindness?
2. What sad event happened when Muhammad ﷺ returned to Makkah?
3. How did Abdul-Muttalib treat Prophet Muhammad ﷺ as a child?

word watch

orphan — يتيم

The class gathered around Teacher Hibah again. They wanted to hear the next part of the beautiful story of Prophet Muhammad ﷺ. They had waited all day to hear more of it.

Teacher Hibah: Let's continue our wonderful story. . .

Muhammad in the Desert

For five happy years, Muhammad lived with Haleemah and her family in the desert. He grew up with Haleemah's children, and they were always good to each other. They all loved each other very much.

Young Muhammad ﷺ brought Haleemah's family many blessings because they took good care of Muhammad ﷺ. Allah gave them more food and water, and the sheep gave more milk. Haleemah was very happy with Muhammad ﷺ and took good care of him. She taught him to be a very good boy.

Muhammad ﷺ Returns to Makkah

When he was six years old, Muhammad ﷺ returned to his mother and grandfather in Makkah. Even though he was sad about leaving Haleemah and her family, young Muhammad ﷺ was very excited to live with his mother and grandfather again.

Aminah Dies

Soon after Muhammad came to Makkah, Aminah wanted to take him to visit his father's grave, and to visit his uncles near Yathrib. But Aminah became sick during the trip and died. Muhammad felt very sad and lonely. He was an orphan. He had lost his father and his mother, and he felt so alone.

Bilal: Mona is crying!
Teacher Hibah: Oh, Mona, my dear, why you are crying?
Mona: I lost my mother when I was a baby, too. It's hard to live without a mother.
Teacher Hibah hugged Mona. Teacher Hibah: I am sorry for you, Mona. Your father is there for you, and the class will take care of you.
Mona: All the other kids here are lucky to have their mothers alive.
Zaid: I am so sad for you, Mona. I never knew how hard it is to lose a father or a mother. When I go back home today, I will hug my dad and mom and pray to Allah to keep them safe for me.
Class: We will all do that.
Teacher Hibah: I am proud of you, children. As good Muslim kids, you should also be kind, nice, and obedient to them.

Healthy habit

Thank Allah for your parents, and always be nice to them.

The Prophet's ﷺ grandfather, Abdul-Muttalib, understood how sad and hurt young Muhammad ﷺ felt, and he took good care of him. Abdul-Muttalib cared very much for his grandson. He knew that Muhammad ﷺ would grow up to be a very special person, and he treated Muhammad ﷺ in a very nice way.

WORDS OF WISDOM
HOLY QUR'AN

سورة الضحى
Surat Ad-Duha

بِسْمِ اللَّهِ الرَّحْمَٰنِ الرَّحِيمِ

وَالضُّحَىٰ ﴿١﴾ وَاللَّيْلِ إِذَا سَجَىٰ ﴿٢﴾ مَا وَدَّعَكَ رَبُّكَ وَمَا قَلَىٰ ﴿٣﴾ وَلَلْآخِرَةُ خَيْرٌ لَكَ مِنَ الْأُولَىٰ ﴿٤﴾ وَلَسَوْفَ يُعْطِيكَ رَبُّكَ فَتَرْضَىٰ ﴿٥﴾ أَلَمْ يَجِدْكَ يَتِيمًا فَآوَىٰ ﴿٦﴾ وَوَجَدَكَ ضَالًّا فَهَدَىٰ ﴿٧﴾ وَوَجَدَكَ عَائِلًا فَأَغْنَىٰ ﴿٨﴾ فَأَمَّا الْيَتِيمَ فَلَا تَقْهَرْ ﴿٩﴾ وَأَمَّا السَّائِلَ فَلَا تَنْهَرْ ﴿١٠﴾ وَأَمَّا بِنِعْمَةِ رَبِّكَ فَحَدِّثْ ﴿١١﴾

TRANSLITERATION

[1] Wadduha
[2] Wallayli itha saja
[3] Ma wadda'aka rabbuka wama qala
[4] Walal-akhiratu khayrul laka min-al-'oola
[5] Walasawfa yu'teeka rabbuka fatarda
[6] Alam yajidka yateeman faawa
[7] Wawajadaka dallan fahada
[8] Wawajadaka 'aa-'ilan fa'aghna
[9] Fa'ammal-yateema fala taqhar
[10] Wa'ammassa-ila fala tanhar
[11] Wa'amma bini'mati rabbika fahaddith

TRANSLATION

[1] By the bright morning
[2] And [by] the night when it covers [the world] with darkness
[3] Your Lord has not left you alone,
[4] And the Hereafter is better for you than the first [life].
[5] And your Lord is going to give to you, and you will be happy.
[6] Didn't He find you an orphan and give you a home?
[7] And He found you lost, then He guided [you].
[8] And He found you poor and gave [you] wealth.
[9] So do not hurt the orphan.
[10] And do not yell at the poor person.
[11] And tell others about the gifts of your Lord.

Healthy habit

Make du'aa for all the orphans around the world and ask Allah to help them. You can help poor orphans, too, by saving your money and giving it to them!

Abdul-Muttalib loved Muhammad ﷺ so much that he even let Muhammad ﷺ sit on his mattress. None of Abdul-Muttalib's own children were allowed to sit on his mattress, only around it. But the Prophet's grandfather insisted that Muhammad sit right next to him.

Allah is Al-Mughni

المغني

All-Giving

Allah is the One Who gives to the poor and the needy until they are satisfied. Allah is the One Who feeds and takes care of all His creatures.

B29

Abdul-Muttalib Dies, Too

The Prophet ﷺ made his grandfather proud of him, because he was a very polite boy. However, Abdul-Muttalib was getting old, and he died when Muhammad ﷺ was eight years old. Now Muhammad ﷺ had also lost his grandfather.

Zaid: This is a very sad story; I did not know that Prophet Muhammad ﷺ went through so many problems when he was a child.

Bilal: What happened next, Teacher?

Teacher Hibah: Prophet Muhammad ﷺ was so sad about losing his grandfather, but Allah helped him through all his troubles. Insha'Allah I will continue this story next time. Right now, just imagine how you would feel if this happened to you, and be thankful that Allah has given you so much.

ACTIVITY TIME

If you can, visit with an orphaned child along with a group of your friends. Have an adult go with you.

WORDS OF WISDOM
HOLY QUR'AN

سورة الماعون
Surat Al-Ma'un

بِسْمِ اللَّهِ الرَّحْمَٰنِ الرَّحِيمِ

أَرَأَيْتَ الَّذِي يُكَذِّبُ بِالدِّينِ ﴿١﴾ فَذَٰلِكَ الَّذِي يَدُعُّ الْيَتِيمَ ﴿٢﴾ وَلَا يَحُضُّ عَلَىٰ طَعَامِ الْمِسْكِينِ ﴿٣﴾ فَوَيْلٌ لِّلْمُصَلِّينَ ﴿٤﴾ الَّذِينَ هُمْ عَن صَلَاتِهِمْ سَاهُونَ ﴿٥﴾ الَّذِينَ هُمْ يُرَاءُونَ ﴿٦﴾ وَيَمْنَعُونَ الْمَاعُونَ ﴿٧﴾

TRANSLITERATION

[1] Ara'ayt -allathee yukaththibu biddeen
[2] Fathalik-allathee yadu'ul-yateem
[3] Wala yahuddu 'ala ta'aam-il-miskeen
[4] Fawaylul-lilmusalleen
[5] Allatheena hum 'an salatihim sahoon
[6] Allatheena hum yura'oon
[7] Wayamna'oon-al-m a'oon

B31

TRANSLATION

[1] Did you see the one who does not believe in the Day of Judgment?
[2] He is the (man) who is harsh with the orphan
[3] And does not encourage others to feed the poor.
[4] We will punish the worshippers
[5] Who neglect their prayers,
[6] Those who just want to show off
[7] And do not help others with their wealth.

Listen to this surah on *Track 5* of your CD.

Healthy habit

When a Muslim goes through tough times and loses a parent or a family member, he or she should be patient, accept Allah's will, and say:

إنّا لِلّه وإنا إليه راجعون

"Inna lillahi wa inna ilayhi raji'oon"

This means: "We belong to Allah, and to Him we return."

CHAPTER REVIEW

ACTIVITY TIME

Write down some of the good things that Allah has given you, and say "Alhamdulillah" for them all the time.

Study questions

1. At what age did Prophet Muhammad ﷺ lose his mother?
2. What does it mean to be an orphan?
3. How should a Muslim treat an orphan, as we learn from Surat Ad-Duha?
4. Who was the grandfather of Prophet Muhammad ﷺ?
5. How old was Muhammad ﷺ when his grandfather died?
6. How did Muhammad ﷺ act during his painful time?

UNIT B CHAPTER 4

The Blessed Young Man

questions?

1. Do you like to take care of animals?
2. Did Prophet Muhammad ﷺ take care of animals?
3. Do you like to travel? Where did the Prophet ﷺ travel to?

word watch

jazakum Allahu khairan	جزاكم الله خيراً
idol	صنم
Abu Talib	أبو طالب

Teacher Hibah gathered the class to talk more about the Seerah of Prophet Muhammad ﷺ.

Teacher Hibah: The Prophet ﷺ had been through many sad times when he was young. But he still behaved very well as he was growing up.

Abu-Talib Takes Care of Muhammad

After Abdul-Muttalib, the Prophet's grandfather, passed away, Muhammad's ﷺ uncle, **Abu Talib**, took him into his care. Abu Talib was a poor man, but he was very kind and generous. He loved Muhammad ﷺ just like he loved his own sons.

Muhammad ﷺ As a Shepherd

Abu-Talib taught Muhammad ﷺ many good things. The Prophet ﷺ was always thankful to his uncle for his kindness. When he was twelve, the Prophet ﷺ chose to become a young shepherd to help his family. As a shepherd, he learned how to be responsible and kind to animals. It was a quiet job outside of Makkah. He had long periods of time to think deeply while breathing the fresh air.

Healthy habit

When a person does something nice for you, say:

جزاكم الله خيراً

"jazakum Allahu khairan."
It means: May Allah bless you with goodness.

A Special Youth

As a young man, Muhammad ﷺ was different from the other youth. He was kind, fair, and he always helped others. He never told a lie or said bad words. This is why everyone loved him. He was always honest. For this, Allah blessed him and made people respect him.

Bilal: Teacher, that means we should always be kind and honest too!

Teacher Hibah smiled: You are very right, Bilal. Muhammad ﷺ was an example for us even before he became a prophet!
Teacher Hibah went on...

A Trip to Syria

Most of the people of Makkah were traders. They bought things from one place and sold them in another.

One day, Abu-Talib decided to go on a trading trip to Syria. Muhammad ﷺ sweetly asked his uncle to take him along. He wanted to see the world around him and learn new things! Abu-Talib agreed.

They traveled and reached a place called Busra, where a Christian priest named Baheera lived. Priest Baheera watched the caravan coming. He noticed a cloud shading the travelers from the sun as they came near his small church. Priest Baheera invited Abu Talib and his group to dinner.

Baheera Meets Muhammad

When Baheera met Muhammad ﷺ, he just loved him, and he asked who Muhammad's ﷺ father was. He learned that Muhammad ﷺ was an orphan. Baheera also saw a birth mark on the shoulder of Muhammad. Baheera then told Abu Talib that a prophet would come soon to Arabia, as the holy books said. The new prophet, he said, "would be an orphan like Muhammad."

"He will also have a mark on his shoulder like the one Muhammad ﷺ has," he added. Priest Baheera begged Abu Talib to protect Muhammad ﷺ very well, all the time. Abu-Talib decided to hurry and get Muhammad ﷺ back home to Makkah for his safety and protection.

Muhammad in the Mountains

As a young man, Muhammad ﷺ spent more and more time thinking about things. He liked to go up to the mountains to think alone.

He did not like it when his people worshipped **idols**, which were made out of stone or wood. He knew that there must be a GREAT creator that made the beautiful world, not stone statues. Idol worshippers thought they were doing the right thing.

Muhammad ﷺ knew that there was much more for him and the people to learn.

WORDS OF WISDOM
HOLY QUR'AN

سورة قريش
Surat Quraysh

بِسْمِ اللَّهِ الرَّحْمَٰنِ الرَّحِيمِ

لِإِيلَافِ قُرَيْشٍ ﴿١﴾ إِيلَافِهِمْ رِحْلَةَ الشِّتَاءِ وَالصَّيْفِ ﴿٢﴾ فَلْيَعْبُدُوا رَبَّ هَٰذَا الْبَيْتِ ﴿٣﴾ الَّذِي أَطْعَمَهُم مِّن جُوعٍ وَآمَنَهُم مِّنْ خَوْفٍ ﴿٤﴾

TRANSLITERATION

[1] Li-eelafi qurayshin
[2] Eelafihim rihlata alshshita-i waalssayf
[3] FalyaAAbudoo rabba hatha albayt
[4] Allathee atAAamahum min jooAAin waamanahum min khawfin

TRANSLATION

[1] For the accustomed security of the Quraysh
[2] Their accustomed security [in] the caravan of winter and summer
[3] Let them worship the Lord of this house,
[4] Who has fed them, [saving them] from hunger and made them safe, [saving them] from fear.

CHAPTER REVIEW

ACTIVITY TIME

1. Draw a caravan of camels.

2. Draw a map of Arabia and point out Makkah and Yathrib.

Study questions

1. Who took care of Prophet Muhammad ﷺ after his grandfather died?

2. How did the Prophet ﷺ try to help out his uncle?

3. What did the people of Makkah do that Muhammad ﷺ disliked?

4. What was Prophet Muhammad's ﷺ first job?

5. Why did the Prophet go up to the mountains?

UNIT B CHAPTER 5

As-Sadiq Al-Ameen: The Truthful, the Trusted

questions?

1. What was the Prophet's job after herding animals?
2. Why did people trust Muhammad ﷺ?
3. What was the big problem he solved?

word watch

| As-Sadiq Al-Ameen | الصادق الأمين |
| Al-Hajar Al-Aswad | الحجر الأسود |

Zaid was very excited. The Seerah stories were more interesting every day! He wanted to find out even more. The Prophet ﷺ had always taught Muslims to love learning, and Mama had taught Zaid to do so, too. His classmates were just as excited, and today, they were sitting around Teacher Hibah's chair even before she got there!

Teacher Hibah walked in and said: Assalamu alaykum, children. Are you ready to continue our special story?
Class: Waalaykum Assalaam, Dear Teacher! Yes, yes, yes! We can't wait!
Teacher Hibah laughed: Let's get started, then. We left off where Abu-Talib was taking care of the Prophet ﷺ as he was growing up. We know he taught the Prophet ﷺ many good things. He also took him on a business trip to Syria.

Let's find out more about our beloved Prophet's life...

Muhammad Becomes a Merchant

As Muhammad ﷺ became a young man, people loved him more and more. They started to call him **As-Sadiq Al-Ameen**, the Truthful, the Trusted. He was kind and honest in everything that he did.

When he was twenty-five, Muhammad ﷺ became a merchant. He sold goods with honesty.

B43

Muhammad ﷺ Solves a Problem

When Muhammad ﷺ was thirty-five, the people of the Quraysh tribe wanted to rebuild Al-Ka'bah. It had almost been ruined in a great flood. When they wanted to place Al-Hajar Al-Aswad, the Black Stone, in the right corner, fights broke out between the chiefs. They all wanted the honor of placing this holy stone in the right place. They began to fight for this job. Our dear Prophet ﷺ was the one who solved this problem.

Now Zaid was curious.

Zaid: Teacher, how did they all agree to listen to Muhammad ﷺ if they were fighting so much?

Teacher Hibah: Good question, Zaid. The oldest of the chiefs came up with a good idea. He proposed that the first one to enter the courtyard would decide who would place Al-Hajar Al-Aswad. Allah made it so that Muhammad ﷺ would enter the masjid first. When he entered, everyone was happy that Muhammad ﷺ was to make the decision! He was As-Sadiq Al-Ameen, so they would trust what he said. Muhammad ﷺ had the chiefs lay down a cloth next to the Black Stone, together. Then, he put the stone in the middle of the cloth. The chiefs lifted the cloth up together with the stone in the middle. Muhammad ﷺ was the one who put the stone in its place after it had been raised. With his solution, Muhammad ﷺ saved everyone from a very scary problem. They were all happy because they all helped put Al-Hajar Al-Aswad in the right place.

Teacher Hibah: See how wise our dear Prophet ﷺ was? He was smart and came up with a very fair way to solve the problem.

Zaid: The Prophet ﷺ was so smart, teacher! I wish I could help people like he did!

Class: We do, too!

Teacher Hibah: He could do that because he was honest and trustworthy. That is why people listened to him. Children, try your best to be like the Prophet, to think and act like him. This is why it is so important for us to learn the Seerah!

Bilal: Thank you so much for teaching us this beautiful story, teacher.

Class: Jazakum Allahu khairan, Teacher Hibah!

Teacher Hibah: Wa'iyyakum insha'Allah.

WORDS OF WISDOM
HOLY QUR'AN

سورة الشرح
Surat Ash-Sharh

بِسْمِ ٱللَّهِ ٱلرَّحْمَٰنِ ٱلرَّحِيمِ

أَلَمْ نَشْرَحْ لَكَ صَدْرَكَ ﴿١﴾ وَوَضَعْنَا عَنكَ وِزْرَكَ ﴿٢﴾ ٱلَّذِىٓ أَنقَضَ ظَهْرَكَ ﴿٣﴾ وَرَفَعْنَا لَكَ ذِكْرَكَ ﴿٤﴾ فَإِنَّ مَعَ ٱلْعُسْرِ يُسْرًا ﴿٥﴾ إِنَّ مَعَ ٱلْعُسْرِ يُسْرًا ﴿٦﴾ فَإِذَا فَرَغْتَ فَٱنصَبْ ﴿٧﴾ وَإِلَىٰ رَبِّكَ فَٱرْغَب ﴿٨﴾

TRANSLITERATION

[1] Alam nashrah laka sadrak
[2] Wawada'na 'anka wizrak
[3] Allathee anqada thahrak
[4] Warafa'na laka thikrak
[5] Fa-'inna ma'-al'usri yusra
[6] Inna ma'a al'usri yusra
[7] Fa-'itha faraghta fansab
[8] Wa-il arabbika farghab

B47

TRANSLATION

[1] Didn't We clear your heart,
[2] And take away your burden,
[3] Which almost did break your back?
[4] And We praised you [in Earth and the Heavens].
[5] So, with every difficulty, there is a relief:
[6] Truly, with every difficulty, there is a relief.
[7] Therefore, when you are done with a good work, work hard on another one.
[8] And turn in love to your Lord.

Healthy h a b i t

1. Be fair and honest, so people will trust you.
2. Try always to solve problems between others.

Nasheed

Al-Hajar Al-Aswad

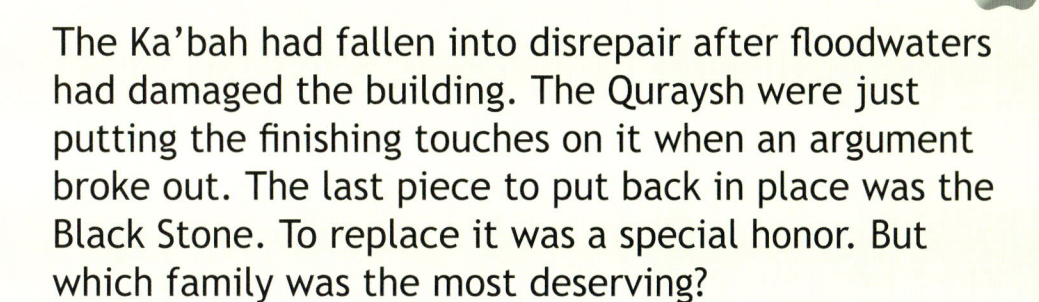

The Ka'bah had fallen into disrepair after floodwaters had damaged the building. The Quraysh were just putting the finishing touches on it when an argument broke out. The last piece to put back in place was the Black Stone. To replace it was a special honor. But which family was the most deserving?

Chorus: "Who will put the Black Stone back in place? Who will be the one to win first place?"
Rich Man: "I am the richest!"
Old Man: "I am the eldest!"
Noble Man: "I am the noblest of our clan!"
Rich Man: "One hundred camels!"
Old Man: "Dozens of servants!"
Noble Man: "Twenty-seven caravans!"
Rich Man: "Who will it be?"
Old Man: "Pick me!"
Noble Man: "No, me!"
Leader: "Wait! We need a helping hand. The first man to enter by the gate will be the one to decide our fate."
Chorus: "Who will put the Black Stone back in place? Who will be the one to win first place?"

The men waited anxiously. Suddenly, footsteps were heard. The crowd eagerly looked up, and when they saw who it was, a cry of delight went up from all the men!

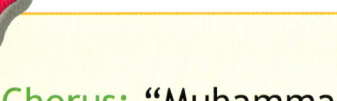

Chorus: "Muhammad!!!
Muhammad is the kindest!
Muhammad is the fairest!
Muhammad is the best in all the land!
Will he pick the richest?
Will he pick the eldest?
Will he pick the noblest of our clan?"

Rich Man: "Who will it be?"
Old Man: "Pick me!"
Leader: "Stop! Let Muhammad take a stand."

Muhammad ﷺ thought for moment and then asked one of the men to run and bring a cloth. He put the Black Stone in the center of the cloth and asked one man from each tribe to pick up an edge of it. On a count of...

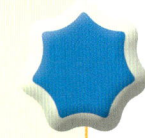

Chorus: "1,2,3!"

..all the men hoisted the cloth, carrying the Black Stone to the Ka'bah. Muhammad ﷺ was given the final honor of putting the Stone in its resting place.

Chorus: "We ALL put the Black Stone back in place. Winners ALL, by Muhammad's grace."

And so with the wisdom that Allah had bestowed on him, Muhammad ﷺ offered a fair and wise solution that satisfied everyone and again won the hearts of his people.

Listen to this nasheed on *Track 10* of your CD.

CHAPTER REVIEW

ACTIVITY TIME

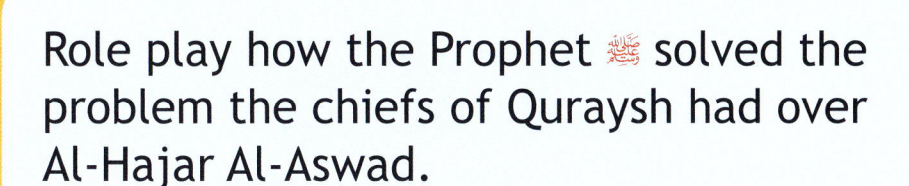

Role play how the Prophet ﷺ solved the problem the chiefs of Quraysh had over Al-Hajar Al-Aswad.

Study questions?

1. How was Al-Ka'bah ruined?
2. What was the big problem they were fighting over?
3. Who came up with the solution to the problem of the Black Stone?
4. How did the chiefs of Quraysh choose Muhammad ﷺ to solve their problem?
5. What did Muhammad ﷺ do to solve the problem?

UNIT B CHAPTER 6 — The Happy Marriage

questions?

1. Who was Muhammad's ﷺ first wife?
2. How did she meet him?
3. How did Muhammad ﷺ feel about his wife?
4. How did they treat each other?
5. What do you know about their family?

word watch

Zaynab	زينب
Ruqayyah	رُقَيَّة
Ummu Kulthum	أم كلثوم
Fatimah	فاطمة
Al-Qasim	القسّام
Abdullah	عبد الله

It was time for Seerah stories again! The children were always excited about hearing more wonderful stories about Prophet Muhammad ﷺ. Teacher Hibah began right away.

Teacher Hibah: We learned last time that when Muhammad ﷺ was a grown man, he worked as a merchant. He was buying and selling goods. Muhammad ﷺ was known for being honest ever since he was a child. He never cheated or lied to any person he worked with.

Muhammad ﷺ always had wonderful manners. He gave all people love and respect. He treated everyone like they were his favorite person! This is why everyone loved Muhammad ﷺ.

Healthy h a b i t

Always treat every person you meet with great respect and love. Even if you don't like someone very much, you should still treat them with care and patience.

Teacher Hibah: Remember that Muhammad ﷺ went to work for a lady named Khadeejah رضي الله عنها.

> We should say "Radi'Allahu 'Anha" رضي الله عنها whenever we hear or say Khadeejah's name. This means "May Allah be pleased with her."

Khadeejah was a very noble lady. She came from a very good family, and she acted in a very nice way. She had been married once, but her husband had passed away. Khadeejah was also a very hard worker.

> Hard work pays off. Khadeejah was very successful and rich. Allah helps hard workers.

Khadeejah had great manners and a good character. Many men wanted to marry her. She did not want to marry any of these men. She wanted someone special.

> Muslim girls and ladies should use Khadeejah as one of their role models. They should learn from the way she acted and from the way she lived.

Khadeejah asked Muhammad ﷺ to go to Syria on a business trip. When he came back, she was surprised. He made so much money for her! Allah had given her great blessings. Muhammad ﷺ had done a great job!

Khadeejah knew that Muhammad ﷺ was a very gentle man. He was more honest and truthful than her other workers. Muhammad ﷺ also respected Khadeejah very much. Khadeejah liked Muhammad ﷺ and wished to marry him. She sent a friend to talk to his family and Muhammad agreed to marry her. Later they got married and loved each other very much.

Teacher Hibah: Muhammad ﷺ was younger than his wife. He was only 25 when they were married, and she was 40!

Khadeejah and Muhammad ﷺ were always nice to each other. They helped each other out through hard times. Muhammad ﷺ respected his wife, and she respected him.

Teacher Hibah: How can we tell if someone respects someone else?
Mona: Respecting means being kind, gentle, and patient with others! It also means listening and paying attention!
Teacher Hibah: Correct!
Bilal raised his hand.
Bilal: Teacher, did they have children?
Teacher Hibah: Yes, Bilal.

Together, Khadeejah and Muhammad ﷺ had four daughters and two sons;
1. Zaynab, 2. Ruqayyah, 3. Ummu Kulthum,
4. Fatimah, 5. Al-Qasim 6. Abdullah.
The sad thing is that all of them died during the Prophet's lifetime, except for Fatimah. Alhamdulillah, they were all Muslim!

Muhammad ﷺ and Khadeejah were wonderful parents. They loved their children very much. Even as parents, they worked as a team.

Bilal: Thank you so much for teaching us this beautiful story, Teacher.

Class: Jazakum Allahu khairan, Teacher Hibah!

Teacher Hibah: Wa iyyakum, My Dears.

CHAPTER REVIEW

ACTIVITY TIME

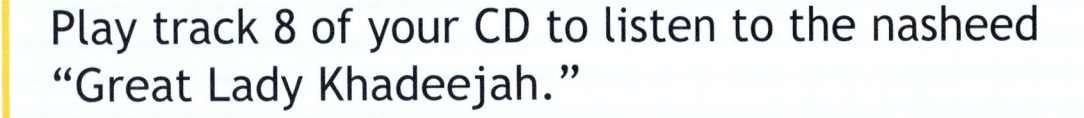

Play track 8 of your CD to listen to the nasheed "Great Lady Khadeejah."

Study questions

1. How did Muhammad ﷺ treat everyone?

2. Describe the great manners of Khadeejah رضي الله عنها.

3. Why did Khadeejah choose to marry Muhammad ﷺ?

4. How did they show respect for each other?

5. How many children did Muhammad ﷺ and Khadeejah have? What are their names?

UNIT B CHAPTER 7

Zaid Bin Harithah
A Young Man Who Loved Muhammad ﷺ

questions?

1. Can anyone love Rasulullah more than he loves his parents?
2. Who was Zaid Ibn Harithah? Whose servant was Zaid?
3. What did the Prophet ﷺ do with Zaid?
4. What happened with Zaid's real parents?

word watch

[Zaid Ibn Harithah   زيد ابن حارثة]

When Zaid came home from school one day, he was sitting with Mama at the table eating his snacks. Mama was going to help him with his homework later. First, she wanted to find out what Zaid had learned at school that day.

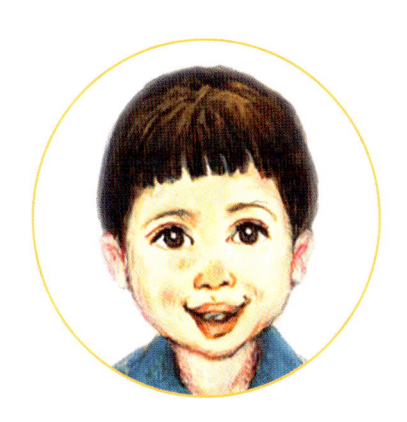

Mama: Zaid, tell me about what you learned at school today.

Zaid: My favorite subject is Islamic studies. Today we learned about the marriage of Khadeejah رضي الله عنها to Muhammad ﷺ. We also learned about how Prophet Muhammad ﷺ solved the problem of Quraysh over Al-Hajar Al-Aswad!

Mama: Stories of the Seerah are always so much fun to hear! We should also learn many lessons from them. Do you know why we named you Zaid? It is a part of the Seerah, but it's a story about another little boy.

Zaid: Wow! Really? Can you please tell me, Mama?
Mama smiled: Of course, Zaid. It's a short story:

Do you know what the name of this boy was?

Hmm...what could it be? Yousuf...Jamal...Ayoob...Salih...Omair...?

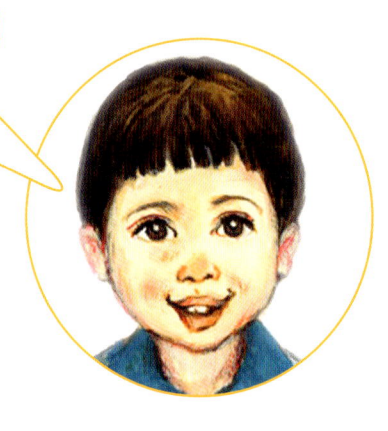

His name was Zaid!

Around the time when Prophet Muhammad ﷺ was a merchant, a mother and her boy were on their way to visit their family.

While they were in the desert, some bad people came on their horses and stole the boy away from his mother. They left her scared and crying. The thieves disappeared in the dust on their running horses. Later, they sold him as a slave in Makkah.

Later on, Khadeejah received this boy as a gift, and when she married Muhammad ﷺ, she gave the boy to Muhammad to serve him.

Zaid: How old was the poor boy, Mama?

Mama: He was eight years old, only a bit older than you.

Mama: The Prophet ﷺ loved the boy very much, so he freed him. He was not a servant anymore, because the Prophet was so kind.

People began to call the boy Zaid Ibn Muhammad, or Zaid the Son of Muhammad ﷺ, but his real name was Zaid Ibn Harithah.

When Zaid's parents found out that their son was with Prophet Muhammad ﷺ, they rushed to get him back. Prophet Muhammad ﷺ did not know that Zaid had been stolen from his parents.

Muhammad ﷺ called Zaid and told him that he could go and live with his parents if he wanted to. Even though Zaid loved his parents, he loved Muhammad ﷺ even more.

So Zaid chose to stay with Muhammad ﷺ and Khadeejah. His parents were sad to leave him, but they were happy that he was with a great person. They knew that Zaid would be well taken care of.

Muhammad

رسولُ الله

Muhammad

Muhammad

Muhammad

Muhammad

Muhammad

B63

WORDS OF WISDOM
HOLY QUR'AN

سورة العاديات
Surat Al-'Adiyat

بِسْمِ ٱللَّهِ ٱلرَّحْمَٰنِ ٱلرَّحِيمِ

وَٱلْعَادِيَاتِ ضَبْحًا ۝١ فَٱلْمُورِيَاتِ قَدْحًا ۝٢ فَٱلْمُغِيرَاتِ صُبْحًا ۝٣ فَأَثَرْنَ بِهِ نَقْعًا ۝٤ فَوَسَطْنَ بِهِ جَمْعًا ۝٥ إِنَّ ٱلْإِنسَانَ لِرَبِّهِ لَكَنُودٌ ۝٦ وَإِنَّهُ عَلَىٰ ذَٰلِكَ لَشَهِيدٌ ۝٧ وَإِنَّهُ لِحُبِّ ٱلْخَيْرِ لَشَدِيدٌ ۝٨ ۞ أَفَلَا يَعْلَمُ إِذَا بُعْثِرَ مَا فِي ٱلْقُبُورِ ۝٩ وَحُصِّلَ مَا فِي ٱلصُّدُورِ ۝١٠ إِنَّ رَبَّهُم بِهِمْ يَوْمَئِذٍ لَّخَبِيرٌ ۝١١

TRANSLITERATION

[1] Wal'aadiyati dabha
[2] Falmooriyati qadha
[3] Falmugheerati subha
[4] Fa-'atharna bihi naq'a
[5] Fawasatna bihi jam'a
[6] Inn-al-'insana lirabbihi lakanood
[7] Wa-'innahu 'ala thalika lashaheed
[8] Wa-'innahu lihubb-il-khayri lashadeed
[9] Afala ya'lamu itha bu'thira ma fil-quboor
[10] Wahussila ma fissudoor
[11] Inna rabbahum bihim yawma-'ithil lakhabeer

TRANSLATION

[1] By the running horses that, with panting (breath),
[2] that are sparking fire [when running on rocks],
[3] And they are raiding in the morning,
[4] And raising the dust,
[5] Then they run into the midst of people
[6] Truly man is ungrateful to his Lord;
[7] And he admits that;
[8] And he loves wealth very much.
[9] Doesn't he know- that when graves are scattered around
[10] And when all secrets of hearts become known
[11] That their Lord is then aware of everything they did?

Listen to this surah on *Track 11* of your CD.

Healthy habit

Follow as much Sunnah of Prophet Muhammad ﷺ as you can. This proves that you love him very much.

Zaid: Subhan'Allah, Mama. Zaid Ibn Harithah loved the Prophet ﷺ even more than his own parents! Does that mean I should love him more than I love you and Baba?

Mama: Yes, that is exactly what it means, My Dear. We should love Prophet Muhammad ﷺ more than we love ourselves!

Zaid: I can't wait to tell all my friends at school how special my name is!

CHAPTER REVIEW

ACTIVITY TIME

What is your name?
Ask your parents why they gave you this name.

If there is a prophet or sahabi that has a name like yours, ask your parents to tell you his or her story.

Study questions

1. Who did Zaid serve before Muhammad ﷺ?
2. Did the Prophet ﷺ keep Zaid as a slave?
3. Did Zaid choose to live with his parents? Why?
4. What did people used to call Zaid?
5. What was Zaid's real name?

UNIT B CHAPTER 8

Prophet Muhammad ﷺ Loves Children

questions?

1. What types of games did the Prophet ﷺ play with children?
2. Who were the Prophet's ﷺ grandsons?
3. Who were Omair and Nughair?
4. What can you do to show your love for the Prophet ﷺ?

word watch

صحابة	sahabah
العبّاس	Al-Abbas
الحَسن	Al-Hasan
الحُسين	Al-Hussayn
سُجود	sujood
عُمَير	Omair

Prophet Muhammad ﷺ loved children just like you very much. He played and laughed with them. They even rode on his back!

The Prophet and His Cousins

Once, Prophet Muhammad ﷺ was playing with his young cousins, the sons of his uncle **Al-Abbas**. He let them race toward him. He said, "Whoever wins will get a prize." The three children ran to him, falling on his back and lap. The Prophet ﷺ hugged and kissed them.

Al-Hasan and Al-Hussayn

When the Prophet's ﷺ grandchildren, Al-Hasan and Al-Hussayn, were little boys, he would play with them and let them climb on his back. He would joke with them and say, "You are riding a good camel!"

B69

Once the Prophet ﷺ was praying. While he was making **sujood**, Al-Hasan and Al-Hussayn climbed on his back. The **sahabah** (friends of the Prophet ﷺ) were worried about him, because his sujood was taking very long. When he finished his prayer, the sahabah asked him why he had taken such a long time making sujood.
The Prophet ﷺ answered, "I didn't want to interrupt their playing."

Once a companion asked the Prophet if he loved Al-Hasan and Al-Hussayn. The Prophet ﷺ said, "How can I not love them? They are my two roses from this world."

Omair and Nughair

Once in Madinah, there was a boy named **Omair** who had a pet bird. The Prophet ﷺ saw Omair playing with the bird and called it "Nughair" to rhyme with the boy's name. Every time the Prophet ﷺ saw Omair he said, "Omair, how is Nughair?" Omair would answer, "He is fine."

One day, the Prophet ﷺ saw Omair crying. He asked him why. Omair said, "My bird, Nughair, has died." The Prophet sat with Omair for a while. HE comforted and played with him.

Zaid: Dad, I love Prophet Muhammad ﷺ. And did you know he loved children like me?

Baba: Yes, Zaid, I love him too. but how can you show that you really love him?

Zaid: I don't know! Can you tell me, Baba?

Baba: You should follow his manners and Sunnah.

Zaid: Can you give some examples?

Baba: Sure! You must obey Allah, pray on time, be honest, respect your parents and elders, be kind to your friends, greet others and smile at them, and help the needy.

Zaid: I will do all these things, insha'Allah, so I can do the things the Prophet ﷺ did.

Baba: There are so many more things. Start with these, and I will tell you about other manners later.

Zaid: Jazakum Allahu khairan, Dad!

Baba: Wa iyyakum, Zaid.

How can you show that you really love Prophet Muhammad ﷺ?

- Obey Allah
- Pray On Time
- Respect Your Parents
- Help The Needy
- Smile At Others
- Be Kind to Friends

Healthy habit

Whenever you hear the Prophet's name, Say:

صلى الله على مُحمد

or

صلى الله عليه وسلّم

"Salla-llahu Ala Muhammad"
or "Salla-llahu Alayhi Wa Sallam."
It means: "O Allah, bless Muhammad"

Say it 10 times in the morning, 10 times before you sleep, and whenever you can.

This shows that you love the Prophet ﷺ, and he will love you even more!

"Salla-llahu Ala Muhammad"

"Salla-llahu Alayhi Wa Sallam"

Nasheed

We Love Muhammad

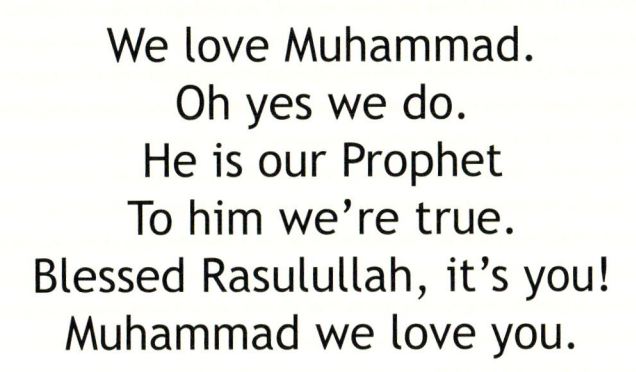

We love Muhammad.
Oh yes we do.
He is our Prophet
To him we're true.
Blessed Rasulullah, it's you!
Muhammad we love you.

We love Muhammad
Sent from Allah.
Was born in Mecca to Aminah.
He was the son of Abdullah.
Muhammad from Allah.

We love Muhammad,
Called "Al Ameen."
He was the greatest man
You've ever seen.
He taught us how to pray
And be clean.
Muhammad Al-Ameen.

Listen to this nasheed on *Track 12* of your CD.

Say this poem out loud with your class!

Poem

O Dear Muhammad

O dear Muhammad, we love you.
You taught us Hadeeth, and Qur'an too.

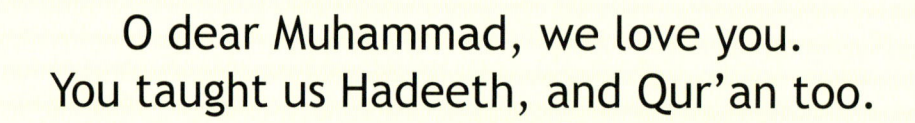

We hope Al-Waseelah is your place,
And to see you in Jannah, face to face.

You were kind so we could see
How a good Muslim should be!

WORDS OF WISDOM
HADEETH SHAREEF

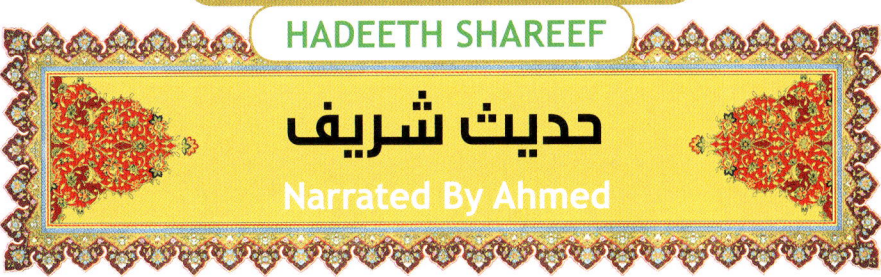

حديث شريف

Narrated By Ahmed

عن عُمر رضي الله عنه: قال رسول الله ﷺ:
"لا يؤمن أحدكم حتى أكون أحبّ إليه من نفسه" رواه أحمد

TRANSLITERATION

"La yo'minu ahadukum hatta akoona ahabba ilayhi min nafsih."

TRANSLATION

Omar رضي الله عنه reported that the Prophet ﷺ said, "You will not be a complete believer until you love me more than yourself."

Study questions

1. How did Muhammed ﷺ have fun with children?
2. What did the Prophet ﷺ do when his grandsons jumped on his back while he was praying?
3. What did Muhammad ﷺ do when Nughair died?
4. How can you show your love for the Prophet ﷺ?
5. What should you do when you hear Muhammad's name?

ادخلوها بسلام آمنين

UNIT C

BORN TO WORSHIP

Chapter 1	The Shining Treasures C2
Chapter 2	Zaid Learns How to Make Wudoo' C12
Chapter 3	Let's Pray! C20
Chapter 4	I Am Seven; I Pray the Right Way C30
Chapter 5	Thikr after Salah C36
Chapter 6	Du'aa: Ask, and You Will Be Answered C46
Chapter 7	Bilal Makes Athan C56
Chapter 8	I Fast in Ramadan................................. C68

UNIT C CHAPTER 1

The Shining Treasures

questions?

1. In what language was Al-Qur'an written?
2. Do you know how Al-Qur'an was revealed? To whom?
3. Why must we read Al-Qur'an?
4. Do you know that Al-Qur'an is full of beautiful stories that teach important lessons?
5. What is the Sunnah?
6. From whom do we learn the Sunnah?

word watch

جبريل	Jibreel
القرآن الكريم	Holy Qur'an
حديث	Hadeeth
أحاديث	Ahadeeth
سورة	surah
سُور	suwar
المُعَوِّذات	Al-Mu'awwithat

Allah sent many books with His prophets to teach people Islam. The **Holy Qur'an** was the last book that Allah sent to people. Allah ordered Angel **Jibreel** to bring Al-Qur'an's words to Prophet Muhammad ﷺ. Prophet Muhammad ﷺ told the people about the Qur'an.

The **Holy Qur'an** has the words and teachings of Allah in Arabic.

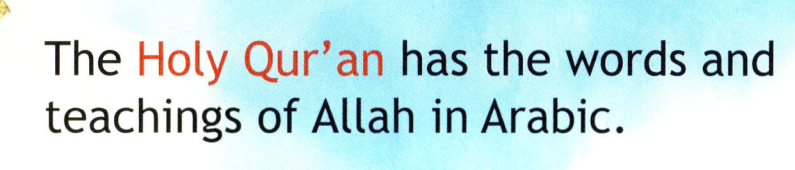

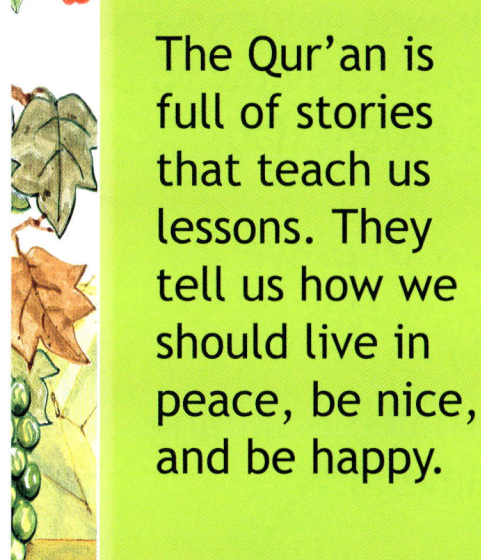

The Qur'an is full of stories that teach us lessons. They tell us how we should live in peace, be nice, and be happy.

Healthy habit

We must read and learn Al-Qur'an every day so that we can become better Muslims.

Allah will be pleased with Muslims who read and practice the Qur'an. The more we read Al-Qur'an, the more hasanat we will get.

For every letter we read of Al-Qur'an, Allah will give us 10 hasanat.

Zaid Finds the Shining Treasures

After dinner one day, Zaid's father was going to the masjid to pray 'Isha. Dad had taught Zaid how to pray, but Zaid wanted to know who had taught dad!

Zaid: Dad, where did you learn how to pray?
Dad: From the shining treasures!

Zaid was about to ask his father what the shining treasures were, but his mother came in.

Mama: Zaid, where are the clothes that you've kept to give to the needy people?
Zaid: I folded them neatly, and I put them in this bag.
Mother: Thank you, Zaid. May Allah reward you for helping the needy ones.
Zaid: Mama, where did you learn about helping others?
Mama: From the shining treasures.

Zaid was about to ask again what the shining treasures were, but it was time to go to pray 'Isha. He was determined to find out what they were.

At bedtime, Zaid read a story with his father. When he finished, he asked Zaid to recite **Al-Mu'awwithat** (Surat Al-Falaq and Surat An-Nas) and his bedtime du'aa.

Zaid: Bismika-llahumma amootu wa ahya! Where did we find this beautiful du'aa Dad?

Dad: From the shining treasures. And it is time for you to go to sleep, Zaid.

Zaid kissed his father goodnight and went to sleep, wondering what the shining treasures were.

When Zaid woke up for Fajr the next day, he found two books at his bedside. The first book was the Holy Qur'an, and the second was a hadeeth book. His father came in with a smile on his face.

Dad: My dear Zaid, you are holding the shining treasures. The Qur'an, My Son, is the word of Allah. It makes us happy, and we shine with iman if we learn and follow Allah's guidance. The Hadeeth book has the sayings and teachings of our Prophet ﷺ .

Zaid was very excited to finally learn about the shining treasures!
Zaid: Dad, how did we get Al-Qur'an?
Dad: Allah revealed it to Prophet Muhammad ﷺ through Angel Jibreel.

The Prophet ﷺ learned Al-Qur'an over 23 years. Each time Angel Jibreel came, the Prophet would learn a surah or a few ayat.

Zaid: What is a surah?
Dad: Surah is a chapter. **Suwar** are many chapters.
Zaid: How many suwar are there in the Qur'an?
Dad: The Qur'an has 114 suwar.
Zaid: What about the Hadeeth?
Dad: A **Hadeeth** is something the Prophet ﷺ said, did or approved, and **Ahadeeth** are more than one Hadeeth. We also call the teachings of the Prophet ﷺ Sunnah.
Zaid: How many Ahadeeth did Rasulullah teach us?
Dad: There are thousands and thousands of Ahadeeth that the companions of the Prophet ﷺ have passed on to us. The two most famous Hadeeth books are Saheeh Al-Bukhari and Saheeh Muslim.

Zaid: Tell me more, Dad!

Dad: As our beloved Prophet ﷺ learned the Qur'an, he memorized everything in it by heart. Then he did everything it said to do. That's why his wife Aisha said, "His behavior was Al-Qur'an."

As Muslims, we don't only learn Al-Qur'an and Hadeeth. We also share them and teach them to others. We also practice their teachings in every day of our lives.

Al-Quran has 114 suwar (chapters)

WORDS OF WISDOM
HADEETH SHAREEF

حديث شريف

Narrated By Bukhari

عن عُثمان بن عفان رضي الله عنه: قال رسول الله ﷺ:
"خَيْرُكم من تعلَّم القرآن وعلَّمه" رواه البخاري

TRANSLITERATION

"Khayrukum man ta'allam-al-Qur'ana wa allamah."

TRANSLATION

Othman Ibn Affan reported that the Prophet ﷺ said, "The best amongst you are those who learn the Qur'an and teach it to others."

WORDS OF WISDOM
HOLY QUR'AN

سورة البينة
Surat Al-Bayyinah

بِسْمِ اللَّهِ الرَّحْمَٰنِ الرَّحِيمِ

لَمْ يَكُنِ الَّذِينَ كَفَرُوا مِنْ أَهْلِ الْكِتَابِ وَالْمُشْرِكِينَ مُنْفَكِّينَ حَتَّىٰ تَأْتِيَهُمُ الْبَيِّنَةُ ﴿١﴾ رَسُولٌ مِنَ اللَّهِ يَتْلُو صُحُفًا مُطَهَّرَةً ﴿٢﴾ فِيهَا كُتُبٌ قَيِّمَةٌ ﴿٣﴾ وَمَا تَفَرَّقَ الَّذِينَ أُوتُوا الْكِتَابَ إِلَّا مِنْ بَعْدِ مَا جَاءَتْهُمُ الْبَيِّنَةُ ﴿٤﴾ وَمَا أُمِرُوا إِلَّا لِيَعْبُدُوا اللَّهَ مُخْلِصِينَ لَهُ الدِّينَ حُنَفَاءَ وَيُقِيمُوا الصَّلَاةَ وَيُؤْتُوا الزَّكَاةَ وَذَٰلِكَ دِينُ الْقَيِّمَةِ ﴿٥﴾ إِنَّ الَّذِينَ كَفَرُوا مِنْ أَهْلِ الْكِتَابِ وَالْمُشْرِكِينَ فِي نَارِ جَهَنَّمَ خَالِدِينَ فِيهَا أُولَٰئِكَ هُمْ شَرُّ الْبَرِيَّةِ ﴿٦﴾ إِنَّ الَّذِينَ آمَنُوا وَعَمِلُوا الصَّالِحَاتِ أُولَٰئِكَ هُمْ خَيْرُ الْبَرِيَّةِ ﴿٧﴾ جَزَاؤُهُمْ عِنْدَ رَبِّهِمْ جَنَّاتُ عَدْنٍ تَجْرِي مِنْ تَحْتِهَا الْأَنْهَارُ خَالِدِينَ فِيهَا أَبَدًا رَضِيَ اللَّهُ عَنْهُمْ وَرَضُوا عَنْهُ ذَٰلِكَ لِمَنْ خَشِيَ رَبَّهُ ﴿٨﴾

TRANSLITERATION

[1] Lam yakun-il-latheena kafaroo min ahl-il-kitabi walmushrikeena munfakkeena hatta ta'tiyahum-ul-bayyinah
[2] Rasoolum-minallahi yatloo suhufam mutahhara
[3] Feeha kutubun qayyimah
[4] Wam atafarraq-al-latheena 'ootul kitaba illa mim ba'di ma ja'at-hum-ul-bayyinah
[5] Wama 'omiroo illa liya'budo-llaha mukhliseena lah-ud-deena hunafa'a wayuqeemo-ssalata way'uto-zzakata wathalika deen-ul- qayyimah

[6] Inna-llatheena kafaroo min ahl-il-kitabi walmushrikeena fee
nari jahannama khalideena feeha 'ola'ika hum sharr-ul-bariyyh
[7] Inn-alla theena amanoo wa'amilo-ssa lihati 'ola'ika hum khayr-ul-bariyyah
[8] Jaza'ohum 'inda rabbihim jannatu 'adnin tajree min tahtiha- anharu khalideena feeh aabadar radiy-Allahu 'anhum waradoo 'anhu thalika liman khashiya rabbah

TRANSLATION

[1] Those who reject (truth), among the People of the Book and among the pagans, were not going to depart (from their ways) until there should come to them clear evidence-
[2] A messenger from God, rehearsing scriptures kept pure and holy:
[3] In it are laws that are right and straight.
[4] Nor did the People of the Book split apart, until after there came to them clear evidence.
[5] And they have been commanded no more than this: To worship God faithfully, be true (in faith); to pray; and to give charity. That is the right religion.
[6] Those who reject (truth), among the People of the Book and among the pagans, will be in Hellfire, to stay there. They are the worst of creatures.
[7] Those who have faith and do good deeds- they are the best of creatures.
[8] Their reward is with God: Gardens of Eternity, beneath which rivers flow; they will stay there forever; God will be pleased with them, and they will be pleased with Him: all this for those who fear their Lord.

Nasheed

Holy Qur'an

Dear little Muslims, have you heard
There is a book known as Allah's word?

Yes, we are Muslims and we've heard
There is a book known as Allah's word.

Dear little Muslims, did you know
Allah revealed it long ago?

Yes, we are Muslims and we know
Allah revealed it long ago.

Dear little Muslims, it's for you
Gives peace and guidance your whole life through.

Yes, we are Muslims and it's true
Gives peace and guidance our whole life through.

Dear little Muslims, take a look
Tell me the name of this Holy Book.

"The Holy Qur'an!"

Listen to this nasheed on Track 13 of your CD.

CHAPTER REVIEW

ACTIVITY TIME

1. Sit down with your parents and read some of the suwar (chapters) of Al-Qur'an.

2. Look for the books of Saheeh Al-Bukhari and Saheeh Muslim. Try to read one Hadeeth from each book.

Study questions

1. Whose words are in the Qur'an?
2. What does Al-Qur'an teach us?
3. Who brought the Qur'an from Allah to the Prophet ﷺ?
4. What are Ahadeeth?
5. Where did the Prophet ﷺ learn how to behave so well?
6. Write your favorite short surah in Arabic.

UNIT C CHAPTER 2

Zaid Learns How to Make Wudoo'

questions?

1. What should you do before prayer?
2. What is wudoo'?

word watch

wudoo': ablution   وُضوء
niyyah: intention   نِيَّة

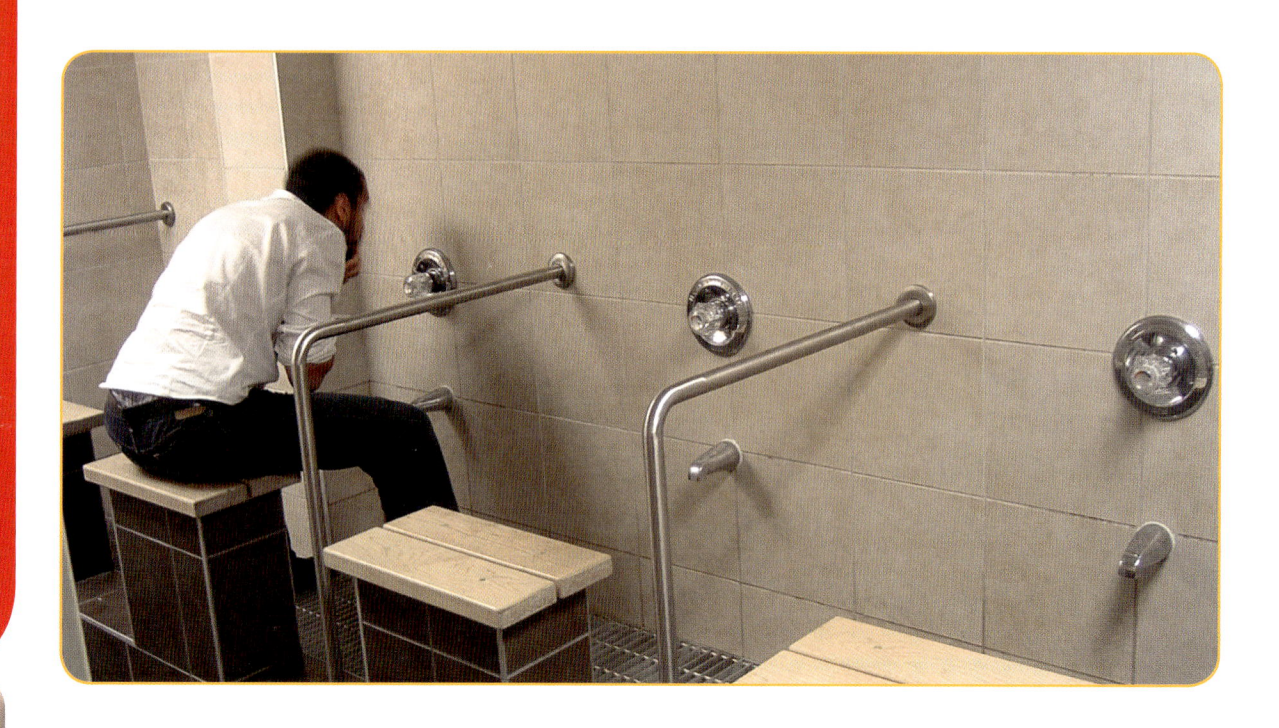

C12

WORDS OF WISDOM
HOLY QUR'AN & HADEETH SHAREEF

قرآن كريم وحديث شريف

بِسْمِ ٱللَّهِ ٱلرَّحْمَٰنِ ٱلرَّحِيمِ

﴿ يَٰٓأَيُّهَا ٱلَّذِينَ ءَامَنُوٓاْ إِذَا قُمْتُمْ إِلَى ٱلصَّلَوٰةِ فَٱغْسِلُواْ وُجُوهَكُمْ وَأَيْدِيَكُمْ إِلَى ٱلْمَرَافِقِ وَٱمْسَحُواْ بِرُءُوسِكُمْ وَأَرْجُلَكُمْ إِلَى ٱلْكَعْبَيْنِ ﴾ المائدة ٦

TRANSLATION

O you who have believed, when you rise to perform prayer, wash your faces and your forearms to the elbows, and wipe over your heads, and wash your feet to the ankles.

عن أبي هريرة رضي الله عنه: قال رسول الله ﷺ :

"لا يقبلُ اللهُ صلاةَ أحدِكم إذا أحدَثَ حتّى يتَوضَّأ" رواه أحمد

TRANSLATION

Abu Hurayrah narrated that the Prophet ﷺ said, "God will not accept your prayer if you use the bathroom, unless you make wudoo'."

Reported by Al-Bukhari and Muslim

C13

Story Time

Zaid is a second grader. He loves to come to school and learn new things every day. During Islamic studies class, the teacher wanted to review wudoo'. She said that this week their lesson would be about how to make wudoo'. "What is wudoo'?" asked Zaid. "**Wudoo'** is washing some parts of the body (hands, face and feet, among others) to get ready for prayer," said the teacher.

At the end of class, the teacher gave the students an assignment. She asked them to go home and practice making wudoo' with their parents. Zaid was so glad to learn about wudoo'. He told his parents about his assignment.

Zaid's father told him, "Having wudoo' is like entering the door to salah. Salah will not be correct if wudoo' is not done." Lena, Zaid's sister, a third grader, asked him, "Would you like me to help you make wudoo'?" "Would you really help me? Thanks, Lena," Zaid said.

CONSERVE... DO NOT WASTE WATER

Remember while making wudoo' to use a small amount of water. Do not leave the water running while you are talking with others. There are many parts of the world that are missing the clean running water that you have. Be thankful to Allah for this water by conserving it. Let's read the following story together:

NOT EVEN FROM A RUNNING RIVER

Once the Prophet ﷺ was walking by when he saw a sahabi named Sa'ad making wudoo'. He was using too much water. The Prophet ﷺ taught Sa'ad that he shouldn't waste water, even if he were making wudoo' at a running river.

WHAT MAKES YOU LOSE AND BREAK YOUR WUDOO'?

1 Using the toilet.

2 Passing gas.

3 Falling asleep.

C15

Let us learn the steps of wudoo', just like Zaid did:

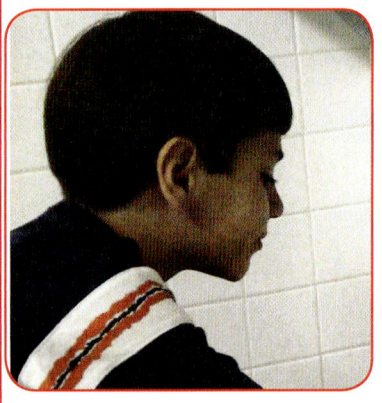

1 Make intention of making wudoo' in your heart (**niyyah**).

2 Wash both hands to the wrists, starting with the right hand.

3 Rinse your mouth three times with water, and spit the water out.

4 Clean your nose with water three times.

5 Wash your face three times.

6 Wash your right arm then your left arm to the elbow, three times.

7 Wipe your head once.

8 Wash your right foot, then your left foot, three times.

C17

WHEN I FINISH WUDOO' I RECITE THIS DU'AA:

أشهدُ أنْ لا إله إلا الله وحده لا شريك له
وأشهدُ أنّ مُحمداً عَبْدُه ورسوله

I bear witness there is no god but Allah,
That He is One with no partner,
And I bear witness that Muhammad is
His servant and messenger.

Did you know?

The Prophet ﷺ told us that when someone makes wudoo', his sins leave his body.

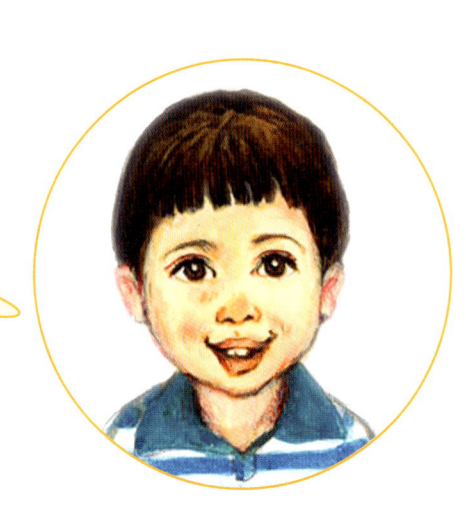

CHAPTER REVIEW

ACTIVITY TIME

1. Create a poster that explains how a Muslim boy or girl can perform wudoo'.

2. Go to the masjid with your parents and perform wudoo' there.

Study questions

1. What does the word wudoo' mean?

2. Recall the ayah on wudoo'.

3. Does Allah accept salah without wudoo'? Support your answer with a Hadeeth.

4. What do we say in our heart before we start wudoo'?

5. What statement do we say when we start wudoo'?

6. What statement do we say when we finish wudoo'?

7. What do we do during wudoo'?

8. What are the things that break wudoo'?

UNIT C CHAPTER 3

Let's Pray!

questions?

1. Do you know what is one of the keys to Paradise (Al-Jannah)?
2. How important is prayer in our daily lives?
3. How can you avoid making mistakes during prayer?
4. What can you do to sit beside Prophet Muhammad ﷺ on the Day of Judgment?

word watch

[
salah: prayer صلاة
niyyah: intention نيّة
rukoo': bowing رُكوع
sujood: prostration سُجود
At-Tahiyyaat: prayer during juloos التّحيّات
]

Main Idea:

Praying five times a day is one of the five pillars of Islam. One should take care of prayer and enjoy it. Prayer gives strength to your soul, as food gives strength to your body!

WASH YOUR SINS AWAY!

قال رسول الله ﷺ:

"لو أنَّ نهراً بباب أحدكم يغتسلُ فيه كلَّ يوم خمسَ مرّات، هل يبقى من دَرَنه شيء؟ قالوا: لا يبقى من دَرَنه شيء، قالوا: فذلك مَثَلُ الصَّلوات الخَمسِ يمْحُ الله بهنَّ الخَطايا."

رواه البخاري ومسلم والبيهقي

The Prophet ﷺ said, "If a river runs in front of your door, and you bathe in it every day five times, would you have any dirt left?" They said, "No dirt would be left." He said, "That is the example of the five prayers; Allah erases the sins with them."

Narrated by Al-Bukhari, Muslim and Al-Bayhaqi

Do you know what is the key to Jannah?

قال رسول الله ﷺ:

"مِفْتاحُ الجَنَّة الصَّلاة"

رواه أحمد وابن ماجه

The Messenger of Allah said:
"The key to Paradise is prayer."
Narrated by Ahmed and ibn Majah

C21

think about it!

Have you tried to turn on the TV without having the plug in first?
Surely, the light will not come on, because the plug is not connected to the electricity.

Did you know?

Prayer, **salah**, is your connection with Allah سبحانه وتعالى.

﴿ قُلْ إِنَّ صَلَاتِي وَنُسُكِي وَمَحْيَايَ وَمَمَاتِي لِلَّهِ رَبِّ ٱلْعَٰلَمِينَ ۝ ﴾ الأنعام ١٦٢

"Say indeed my prayer, my sacrifice, my living, and my dying are for Allah, Lord of the Worlds."

Surat Al-An'aam 162

Beware of thieves!!

Can Shaytan steal from your prayer?

Prophet Muhammad ﷺ was asked about turning one's face during prayer. He replied, "That is the stealing of Shaytan, in which he steals during the person's prayer." (Bukhari)

The Prophet ﷺ said, "The worst thief is the one who steals from his prayer." He was asked to explain. He said, "He will not complete his rukoo' and his sujood." (Imam Ahmad)

Choose your own salah grade

The more you are focused and practicing humbleness, the higher grade you will receive from Allah سبحانه وتعالى. Let's read the following Hadeeth of the Prophet ﷺ.

The Prophet ﷺ said,
" When a person does his prayer, it will only be written for him one third (of the reward), or one fourth, or half, or one sixth, or one eighth, or one tenth. Therefore, a Muslim is rewarded for his prayer according to the level of his humbleness in it. (Imam Ahmad)

Extra! Extra!

Read all about it!
When praying one of the five daily prayers, you will be rewarded for ten prayers! So remember, when praying your five daily prayers, you just received the reward of fifty prayers. And that is every day!

Ways to help you make your five daily prayers:

1. Use the buddy system by having you and your friends remind one another.
2. Ask your parents to remind you and pray jama'ah together.
3. Make your intention to try your best to pray the five daily prayers.

Did you know: That during sujood you are the closest to Allah سبحانه ?

Did you know: That every time you make sujood, Allah سبحانه وتعالى takes away one sayi'ah and gives you one hasanah?

Subhana Rabiyal A'la
Glory be to my Lord, the Most High!

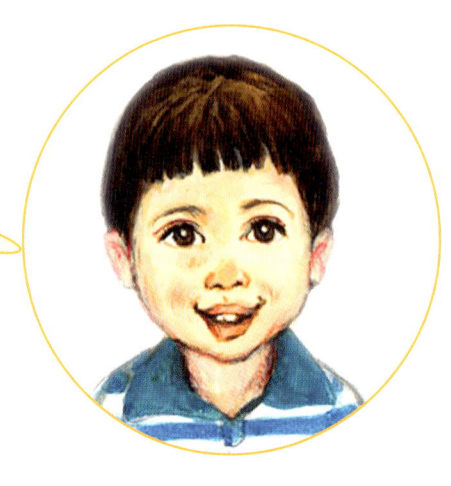

Story Time

Rabi'ah Ibn Ka'b

Once a young sahabi (a friend of the Prophet ﷺ) named Rabi'ah bin Ka'b asked the Prophet ﷺ to be with him in Jannah. Rabi'ah was 14 years old. The Prophet ﷺ asked him, "Is there anything else you want, Rabi'ah?" Rabi'ah answered, "No. All I want is to be with you in Jannah." Then the Prophet ﷺ said:

"فأعني على نفسك بكثرة السّجود"

رواه الطبراني

"Then help yourself by making plenty of sujood."

Are you ready?

After reading about all the great rewards of praying the five daily prayers, are you ready to learn how is it done? Lets learn together:

1 I face the qiblah, Al-Ka'bah in Makkah, and make **niyyah** (intention) in my heart.

2 I raise my hands behind my ears and say "الله أكبر" "Allahu Akbar" (Allah is Great).

3 I read Surat Al-Fatihah and a short surah.

4 I say "الله أكبر" "Allahu Akbar," then make **rukoo'** (bow).

C25

5 During rukoo', I say " سبحان ربي العظيم ", "Subhana Rabiyal-Atheem" (Glory to Allah the Great) 3 times.

6 I rise from rukoo' and say " سمع الله لمن حمده ", "Sami'a Allahu Liman Hamidah" (Allah hears those who praise Him).

7 I say " الله أكبر ", "Allahu Akbar," and then make **sujood** by putting my forehead on the floor. I say " سبحان ربّي الأعلى ", "Subhana Rabiyal-A'la" (Glory to Allah the Most High)

8 I sit up from sujood while saying " الله أكبر ." Then I repeat sujood again.

I just completed one full rak'ah.

9 To start the second rak'ah, I stand up, read Surat Al-Fatihah, and repeat the same steps.

10 After I finish the second rak'ah, I sit down to read **At-Tahiyyaat** and the Ibraheemiyyah prayer.

11 I turn my face to the right side and say: " السّلام عليكم ورحمة الله ," "Assalamu Alaykum wa Rahmatullah" (Peace be upon you and the Mercy of Allah).

12 I turn my face to the left side and say: " السّلام عليكم ورحمة الله " "Assalamu Alaykum wa Rahmatullah"

I have finished two rak'aat now.

C27

التشهُّد / At-Tashahhud

التحيات لله والصلوات والطيبات. السلام عليك أيها النبي ورحمة الله وبركاته. السلام علينا وعلى عباد الله الصالحين. أشهد أن لا إله إلا الله وحده لا شريك له. وأشهد أن محمداً عبده ورسوله.

At-Tahayyatu lillahi wassalawatu wattayyibat, Assalamu 'alayka 'ayyuha-nnabiyyu warahmatullahi wabarakatuh,
Assalamu 'alayna wa 'ala ibad-illahi-ssaliheen,
Ashahadu 'alla 'ilaha illAllah wahdahu la sharica lah
wa 'ash-hadu anna Muhammadan 'abduhu wa rasooluh

الصلاة الإبراهيمية / As-Salat Al-Ibraheemiyyah

اللهم صلِّ على محمد وعلى آل محمد. كما صليت على إبراهيم وعلى آل إبراهيم. وبارك على محمد وعلى آل محمد. كما باركت على إبراهيم وعلى آل إبراهيم. في العالمين. إنك حميد مجيد.

Allahumma salli 'ala Muhammad wa 'ala aali Muhammad
Kama sallayta 'ala Ibraheem wa 'ala aali Ibraheem wa barek 'ala Muhammad wa 'ala aali Muhammad
Kamabarakta 'ala Ibraheem wa 'ala aali Ibraheem
Fi-l'aalameen, innaka hameedun majeed

Healthy habit

When it is time to pray, be the one to remind your friends to get ready for it!

CHAPTER REVIEW

ACTIVITY TIME

1. Create a poster that explains how a Muslim boy or girl can perform Salat al-Fajr.

2. Write At-Tahiyyaat and As-Salat Al-Ibraheemiyyah.

Study questions

1. What does the word salah mean?
2. How does salah clean our souls? Recall a hadeeth that explains this point.
3. Does Allah accept all our salah, even when we do not pray the right way?
4. What did the Prophet say to Rabi'ah ibn Ka'b?
5. Toward where should we face when we pray?
6. What do we say in our heart before we start prayers?
7. What statement do we say when we start prayers?
8. What do we recite as we stand during prayers?

UNIT C CHAPTER 4

I Am Seven; I Pray the Right Way

questions?

1. Do you know what the key to Jannah is?
2. Why is it important to pray the right way?
3. What are some mistakes that people make in their salah?
4. Why is it important to make your prayer perfect?

word watch

[khushoo' خُشوعْ]

Mona was playing with her two-year-old sister when she remembered that it was time to pray 'Asr. Ever since she was little, her father had been teaching her about salah. Now, she was seven years old and could pray all by herself.

She told her sister, "Come on, Maha, let's go pray!" Then she ran to the bathroom to make wudoo'. Maha toddled behind her. As soon as she was finished, she found a prayer rug to use. Mona made sure she was facing the qiblah, just like her father had shown her.

Then she stood up, made her niyyah in her heart, and began her prayer. Maha always followed her big sister, so she tried to act just like her in salah. Mona took her time in her fard prayers, and then sat down to make tasbeeh. But Maha still wanted to pray more!

Mona giggled as she watched her sister trying to pray. She was making sujood in a silly way.

Mona bent down in sujood to show her sister the proper way to make sujood.
"Like this, Maha!" Mona made sure her forehead, her nose, and her knees and toes were touching the ground. Maha started wiggling around, and Mona laughed.
"Maybe you're too young. Let's wait until you are seven years old," she said, hugging Maha.

Later that night, Mona told her father about praying with Maha. He thought it was funny, and he laughed. Then he said, "I am glad you tried to show Maha the right way to pray, Mona.

It is very important to make your salah perfect. The older you get, the more responsible you are for your prayers.

Let me tell you a story about a man who learned just how important it is."

Story Time

One time, the Prophet ﷺ was sitting with his friends (sahabah) when a man entered the masjid and started making salah. When he finished, he came to greet the Prophet ﷺ.

The Prophet ﷺ told him, "Go and pray again because you did not pray." The man went back and repeated his salah. Again, he rushed through the salah. Then he came back to greet the Prophet ﷺ.

Again, the Prophet ﷺ said, "Go pray again, because you did not pray." He repeated this three times. The man then said, "Oh Prophet of Allah, I do not know any better, so teach me."

The Prophet ﷺ then told the man to make wudoo' the right way, then to make sure he was facing the qiblah toward Makkah. Then he taught him how to do takbeer and say "Allahu Akbar" the right way. Then he told him to recite Al-Fatihah and some Qur'an correctly.

Rasulullah ﷺ said, "When you make rukoo', bend down well and don't rush. Then raise your back up straight and don't rush. Make sujood and take your time, then raise your back up straight and take your time. Do this in all your prayers."

Mona really liked this story. She said, "Wow! This means that prayer doesn't even count if we don't pray right!" Father nodded. "That's what this story tells us, Mona. Allah wants us to pray with khushoo'. **Khushoo'** means to be humble before Allah and focus on your prayer. And even if you are alone, you should always remember that you are standing in front of Allah, and that He is watching and listening to your prayer. Many people ruin their salah because they do not pray the right way."

> "Allah always watches you and hears your salah."

Mona asked, "Father, what kinds of things ruin our salah?" Father answered, "Things like looking around, laughing, moving your hands, moving your feet around, and making extra noises."

In prayer:

- **DO NOT** look around
- **DO NOT** laugh or make noises
- **DO NOT** move your hands and feet

Healthy habit

Always take your time in salah and pray with khushoo'.

CHAPTER REVIEW

Study questions

1. What did Mona do to make sure she did a good job in her salah?

2. Why did the Prophet ﷺ tell the man that he had not prayed three times?

3. What does it mean to pray with khushoo'?

4. What does Allah do when you are praying?

UNIT C CHAPTER 5

Thikr after Salah

questions?

1. What do you do after salah?
2. Is it good to run off right after you finish praying?
3. What is one of the best times to remember Allah?

word watch

Sunnah	سُنّة
thikr	ذِكر
tasbeeh	تَسبيح
Istighfar	استغْفار
Subhan'Allah	سُبحانَ الله
Alhamdulillah	الحمدُ لله
Allahu Akbar	الله أكبر
Al-Muhsi	المُحْصي
salat Al-Sunnah	صلاة السُّنة

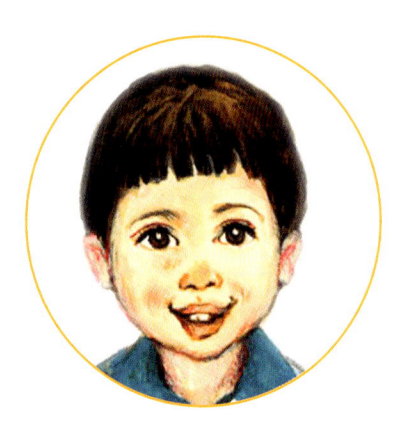

Last week at the masjid, our imam taught us something very important. We were getting up to leave after jama'ah Maghrib prayers, because we wanted to go play on the playground outside...

C36

The imam started speaking about how important it was to sit down and make thikr after salah. He said that we should make istighfar, and say astaghfirullah three times. Then he said we should say tasbeeh. He told us a story about a group of poor people who went to the Prophet ﷺ because they were sad. They could not give charity like the rich people. They thought that the rich people would get a great reward and a high place in Jannah.

The Prophet ﷺ told them that they could get the same reward without spending any money. The Prophet ﷺ told them to say the following after every salah:

Say "SubhanAllah"	سُبحان الله	33 times
Say "Alhamdulillah"	الحَمدُ لله	33 times
Say "Allahu Akbar"	الله أكبر	33 times

C37

So, after the imam taught us this story, we learned that we should say our istighfar and tasbeeh after every salah. Then we will be RICH in good deeds! Imam Luqman also taught us that after we have made the tasbeeh a total of 99 times, we say:

لا إله إلا الله وحده لا شريك له
له الملك وله الحمد وهو على كل شيء قدير

"La ilaha illa Allah wahdahu la Shareeka lah, lahul-mulk, wa lah-ul-hamd, wa howa ala kulli shay'in qadeer"
It means: There is no god but Allah; He has no partner. His is the majesty and praise, and He can do everything."

Healthy **habit**

Always remember to make istighfar and tasbeeh after your salah! You get many hasanat for them!

"The time after salah is a time for thikr and du'aa. We remember how much we love Allah. We thank Allah, and we remember how great, wonderful, and powerful He is. Memorizing the 99 names of Allah will help us to do this."

Allah is AL-MUHSI

المُحصي

THE KNOWER of Counts and Everything Alse.

Allah is the Knower of every single thing in the world. He will know every single tasbeeh or thikr you do, and He will reward you for it.

C40

"We should also remember to recite ayat Al-Kursi after we are done with our tasbeeh, and to make du'aa."

Imam Luqman also told us that out of love and respect for the Prophet ﷺ, we should pray salat Al-Sunnah, or Sunnah prayers. We do them before and after our fard prayers. One special thing about salat Al-Sunnah is that if we make mistakes in our fard prayers, then the Sunnah can make up for these mistakes!

After everyone heard this, everyone stood up to pray Sunnah!

Do you know how many rak'aat of Sunnah prayers to pray for each fard prayer?

Let's remember this:

- Fajr فَجر — 2 Sunnah Before Fajr
- Thuhr ظُهر — 2 or 4 Sunnah Before Thuhr and 2 Sunnah After Thuhr
- 'Asr عَصر — NO Sunnah for 'Asr
- Maghrib مغرب — 2 Sunnah After Maghrib
- 'Isha عِشاء — 2 Sunnah After 'Isha and 3 Rak'aat of Witr

WORDS OF WISDOM
HOLY QUR'AN

سورة قريش
Surat Al-Nasr

بِسْمِ ٱللَّهِ ٱلرَّحْمَٰنِ ٱلرَّحِيمِ

إِذَا جَاءَ نَصْرُ ٱللَّهِ وَٱلْفَتْحُ ۝ وَرَأَيْتَ ٱلنَّاسَ يَدْخُلُونَ فِي دِينِ ٱللَّهِ أَفْوَاجًا ۝ فَسَبِّحْ بِحَمْدِ رَبِّكَ وَٱسْتَغْفِرْهُ إِنَّهُ كَانَ تَوَّابًا ۝

TRANSLITERATION

[1] Itha ja'a nasru-llahi walfat-h
[2] Wara'ayt-an-nasa yadkhuloona fee deen-illahi afwaja
[3] Fasabbih bihamdi rabbika wastaghfirhu innahu kana tawwaba

TRANSLATION

[1] When there comes the help of Allah and the victory,
[2] And you see men entering the religion of Allah in masses,
[3] Then celebrate the praise of your Lord, and ask His forgiveness; surely He forgives after.

Listen to this surah on *Track 14* of your CD.

Nasheed

Remember Allah

Subhan'Allah.
We praise Allah.

Alhamdulillah.
We thank Allah.

Wa la ilaha illa Allah
There is no god but Allah.
Allah is One.

Allahu Akbar.
Allah is Great.

Listen to this nasheed on *Track 15* of your CD.

Healthy habit

Always remember to pray salat Al-Sunnah, or Sunnah prayers! You get many hasanat for them!

CHAPTER REVIEW

Study questions?

1. What is one way Prophet Muhammad ﷺ taught us to become rich?

2. What do you say when you make tasbeeh?

3. What should you think about when you are making thikr?

4. Name two other important things to do after your fard salah.

5. How many Sunnah rak'aat do we pray after Maghrib?

6. How many Sunnah rak'aat do we pray in a day?

C45

UNIT C CHAPTER 6

Du'aa: Ask, and You Will Be Answered

questions?

1. Whom do you turn to for help?
2. What do you do when you are in need?

word watch

[Du'aa دُعاء
Al-Mujeeb المُجيب]

O Allah, to You I pray, throughout the night and the day.

I turn to my Creator, Allah, by making du'aa.

What is " du'aa ?"

Du'aa دُعاء means to ask Allah سُبحانه وتعالى for something. Allah loves those who make du'aa to Him. He told us in Al-Qur'an to ask Him, and He shall answer us.

WORDS OF WISDOM
HOLY QUR'AN

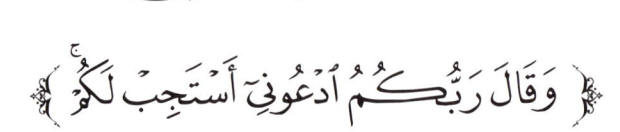

سورة غافر

Surat Ghafir: ayah 60

بِسْمِ اللَّهِ الرَّحْمَنِ الرَّحِيمِ

وَقَالَ رَبُّكُمُ ادْعُونِي أَسْتَجِبْ لَكُمْ

TRANSLITERATION

"Waqala rabbukum ud'ooni astajiblakum"

TRANSLATION

"And your Lord says, "Call upon Me; I will respond to you."

When you call someone many times, he might get bored of you! But when you call upon Allah many times, He will love you more.

Ya Allah, Cure My Son

Bilal came back very tired from school. His mother took his temperature, and it was almost 100 degrees! She took him to the doctor right away. The doctor said he had a throat infection and gave him some medicine.

Bilal's parents were very worried about him. But they remembered that Allah is the only One Who could really cure him and make him feel better. Bilal's parents gave him the medicine and made du'aa for him that night.

In a few days, Bilal was feeling better and up again. The fever was gone. Bilal's parents said, "Alhamdulillah, praise be to Allah, Who answered our du'aa."

"وإذا مَرِضت فهو يَشْفين"

Wa itha maridtu fahowa yashfeen

"When I am sick, He cures me."

Allah is Al-Mujeeb

المجيب

The One Who Answers All.

Manners When Making Du'aa

1. I face the qiblah.
2. I raise up my hands.
3. I start by saying:

الحمد لله رب العالمين والصلاة والسلام على محمد خاتم المرسلين

"Praise be to Allah, and blessings on Prophet Muhammad."

4. I follow the Sunnah of repeating my du'aa 3 times.
5. When I finish making du'aa, I say "Ameen" (O Allah, answer).

What are the best times to make du'aa?

Any time is a good time to make du'aa to Allah, because He hears us all the time. But there are certain times when du'aa is more accepted, such as the following times:

1. After each of the five daily prayers.
2. Between athan and iqamah.
3. During sujood.
4. During rainfall.
5. While a person is fasting.
6. Laylat al-Qadr (the night in Ramadan when the Qur'an was revealed).
7. When you make du'aa for others while they are not with you.
8. When you are traveling.

What happens after you make du'aa?

When you make du'aa to ask Allah something, one of the following things will happen:

1. Allah will give you what you asked for.
2. Allah will give you hasanat on the Day of Judgment, when you might really need it.
3. Allah will protect you from some harm that was going to happen to you.
4. Allah will give you something that is better for you.

Rain, Rain, Come Our Way

Once, a group of hujjaj traveled to Makkah to perform Hajj. The weather was very dry, and people hoped that it would rain. The imam was making a special du'aa asking Allah to give them rain. As soon as the imam finished his du'aa, it started raining.

Healthy habit

Make du'aa to Allah as much as you can.

Let's make du'aa دُعاء together:

- Alhamdulillah, wassalatu wassalamu ala Rasulullah
- Ya Allah, protect my parents from any harm.
- Ya Allah, help me to be the best Muslim.
- Ya Allah, protect my brothers and sisters all around the world. Shelter them, feed them, and keep them safe.
- Ya Allah, we ask Your mercy on those who are living and those who are dead.
- Ya Allah, forgive our sins and grant us Your Jannah.

Ameen

GREAT DU'AA

ربنا آتنا في الدنيا حسنة وفي الآخرة حسنة وقنا عذاب النار

"Rabbana atina fiddunya hasanah, wa fil akhirati hasanah, wa qina athab an-nar"

"Our Lord, give us in this world [that which is] good, and in the Hereafter [that which is] good, and protect us from the punishment of the Fire."

Al-Baqarah: ayah 201

Healthy habit

Always make du'aa to Allah:
- In the morning
- After prayers
- When you need something from Allah
- Before you sleep

Nasheed

Du'aa

Ya Allah, we pray to You
In all we say, in all we do.
Please keep us humble, forever true.
Straight on the path that leads to You.

Ya Allah, with You we'll stay.
Never let Shaytan lead us astray.
Keep our hearts open, show us the way,
Praising You each and every day.

Ya Allah, all praise for You.
Blessings upon our Prophet, too.
Thank You for making us Muslims true,
Worshipping One and only You!

Listen to this nasheed on Track 16 of your CD.

WORDS OF WISDOM
HADEETH SHAREEF

حديث شريف

Narrated By Tirmithi & Abu Dawood

عن النعمان بن بشير: قال رسول الله ﷺ:
"الدُّعاء هو العِبادة" رواه الترمذي وأبو داود

TRANSLITERATION

"Ad-Du'aa Howal Ibadah"

TRANSLATION

An-Nu'man Ibn Basheer reported: The Prophet ﷺ said, supplication is worship."

CHAPTER REVIEW

Study questions

1. What does du'aa mean?
2. Why is du'aa important?
3. When are the best times to make du'aa?
4. How might Allah answer our du'aa?
5. Recite an ayah about the importance of du'aa.
6. Recite a Hadeeth about the importance of du'aa.

UNIT C CHAPTER 7

Bilal Makes Athan

questions?

1. What is the athan?
2. Why do we say the athan?
3. What is the iqamah?
4. Would you like to learn the athan?

word watch

athan	أذان
mu'athin	مُؤَذِّن
iqamah	إقامة

What is the "Athan"?

Athan is the call for prayer. It is a reminder for people to get ready and come to the masjid for salah. It also makes people remember Allah.

Do you know who a "mu'athin" is?

A **mu'athin** is a person who calls the athan. His job is to remind people to get ready for salah. He calls athan five times a day in a loud voice. A long time ago the mu'athin used to climb to the top of the minaret, or the roof of the masjid, and do the athan there.

A minaret is a special tower of the masjid that is made for athan. This way, everyone around the masjid will hear the mu'athin and know that the salah time has started. Today, most masajid have microphones and loudspeakers, so the mu'athin does the athan into the microphone in the masjid. His voice can be heard around the masjid through the loudspeakers.

When the mu'athin is saying the athan, he faces the qiblah, and he raises his hands to his ears.

It has been done this way since the time of the Prophet ﷺ.

We Muslims follow the way taught by him in all parts of our religion.

Bilal ibn Rabah
was the first mu'athin ever!

Bilal's First Athan

Bilal loved to go to the masjid with his father for prayer. Bilal liked to hear the athan in the masjid. "Would you show me how to make the athan, Dad?" asked Bilal. "Of course, Son," said Bilal's dad. Bilal began learning the meaning of the words of the athan. And every day he memorized a few lines of it.

One day, Bilal went to the masjid with his dad. He was waiting with his dad for the athan to be made. The Imam saw Bilal and called to him:

Imam: Assalamu Alaykum. What is your name, Son?

Bilal: Wa Alaykum Assalam. My name is Bilal.

Imam: Masha Allah, your name is like the name of Bilal Ibn Rabah, the first mu'athin in Islam. Would you like to be a Mu'athin like him?

Bilal: Yes.

Imam: Do you know how to say the athan?

Bilal: Yes, my dad taught me that last week.

Imam: Great! Would you like to say it now?

Bilal was surprised; he looked at his dad to see what he should do. His dad smiled and nodded.

Bilal: Yes, I will do it, but I might make some mistakes.

Imam: That is all right, Son. I will correct you if you do.

Bilal stood and faced the qiblah. He was nervous, because it was his first time to make the athan in the masjid.

Bilal raised his hands to his ears and started to make the athan. Every time he said a verse, the imam and the people in the masjid would repeat the same verse after him in a low voice. The imam kept saying, "Masha'Allah, go on Bilal. You are doing just fine." Bilal made only one or two little mistakes, which the imam corrected.

After he finished, the imam and the people made a du'aa of the athan. Then everybody thanked Bilal and encouraged him. One person said, "You have such a beautiful voice, masha'Allah." His father was also proud of him. When Bilal and his dad returned home, they told the family what had happened in the masjid. His mom hugged him, and everyone was very proud of him.

LET US MAKE ATHAN

Would you like to learn the words of athan and their meaning, like Bilal?

اللهُ أَكْبَرْ
"Allahu Akbar"
(Allah is Greater) [4 times]

أَشْهَدُ أَنْ لا إله إلَّا الله
"Ash'hadu An La Ilaha Illa Allah"
("I witness there is no god but Allah")
[2 times]

أَشْهَدُ أَنَّ مُحمداً رَسولُ الله
"Ash'hadu Anna Muhammada Rasulullah"
("I witness that Muhammad is the Messenger of Allah") [2 times]

حَيِّ عَلى الصّلاة
"Hayya Alassalah"
("Come to prayer") [2 times]

حَيِّ عَلى الفَلاحْ
"Hayya Alal Falah"
("Come to success") [2 times]

اللهُ أَكْبَرْ
"Allahu Akbar"
("Allah is Greater") [2 times]

لا إله إلَّا الله
"La Ilaha Illa Allah"
("There is no god but Allah") [1 time]

C61

اللهُ أَكْبَرُ	اللهُ أَكْبَرُ
أَشْهَدُ أَنْ لا إِلهَ إِلاَّ الله	أَشْهَدُ أَنْ لا إِلهَ إِلاَّ الله
أَشْهَدُ أَنَّ مُحمداً رَسولُ الله	أَشْهَدُ أَنَّ مُحمداً رَسولُ الله
حَيِّ عَلى الصَّلاة	حَيِّ عَلى الصَّلاة
حَيِّ عَلى الفَلاحْ	حَيِّ عَلى الفَلاحْ
اللهُ أَكْبَرُ	اللهُ أَكْبَرُ

لا إِلهَ إِلاَّ الله

THE DU'AA OF ATHAN

After the athan is made, Muslims make a du'aa. They say:

اللّهُمّ رب هذه الدّعوة التّامة والصلاة القائِمة

آتِ مُحمداً الوسيلة والفضيلة

وابْعَثْه مَقاماً محموداً الذي وَعَدْته

"Allahumma rabba hathihi-da'wati-tammah wassalatil qa'imah aati Muhammadan al-waseelata wal fadeelah, wab'ath-hu maqaman mahmoodan allathi wa'adtah."

"O Allah, the Lord of all supplications and steadfast prayer, grant Muhammad the most favored and excellant position. Admit him to the praised worthy place that You have promised him."

C63

What is the "iqamah"?

The iqamah is a fast and short call to prayer. We say it right when we are about to start salah.

What is the difference between athan and iqamah?

The athan and iqamah are very similar. The only difference is after saying "Hayya Alal Falah" you add قَدْ قَامَتْ الصَّلاة "qad qamat-is-salah" [2 times]. This means, "Salah has indeed started."

اللهُ أَكْبَرْ اللهُ أَكْبَرْ	One or Two Times
أَشْهدُ أَنْ لا إله إلاَّ الله	One or Two Times
أَشْهدُ أَنَّ مُحمداً رَسولُ الله	One or Two Times
حيِّ عَلى الصّلاة	One or Two Times
حيِّ عَلى الفَلاحْ	One or Two Times
قَدْ قَامَتْ الصّلاة قَدْ قَامَتْ الصّلاة	One Time
اللهُ أَكْبَرْ اللهُ أَكْبَرْ	One Time
لا إله إلاَّ الله	One Time

Prophet Muhammad ﷺ taught us to make du'aa between the athan and the iqamah. We should ask Allah سبحانه وتعالى for forgiveness at this time. The Prophet ﷺ told us that Allah سبحانه وتعالى will answer the du'aa that is made during that time. Don't waste that special time by talking to your friends!

This is the order of events before prayer:

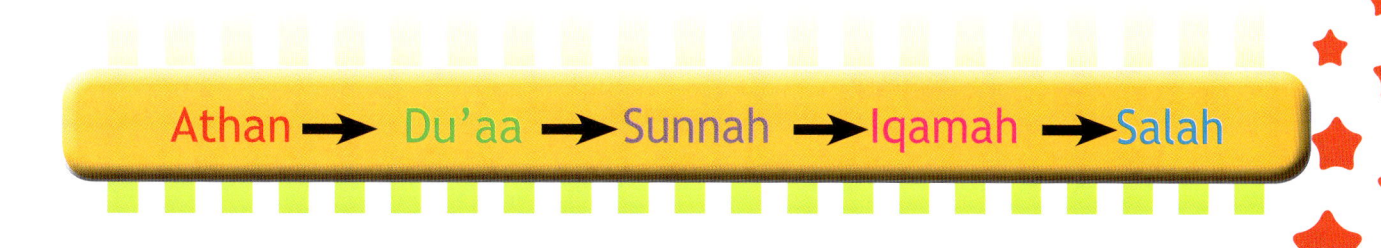

Athan ➡ Du'aa ➡ Sunnah ➡ Iqamah ➡ Salah

WHAT SHOULD WE SAY DURING THE ATHAN?

During the athan, we should repeat what the mu'athin says, except when he says "Hayya As-Salah" and "Hayya Alal Falah." We do not repeat the same thing. Instead we say:

$$\text{لا حَوْلَ وَلا قُوَّة إلاّ بِاللّٰه}$$

"La Hawla Wala Quwata Illa Billah"
"There is no strength or power except with Allah."

A TREASURE FROM JANNAH

Did you know that "La Hawla Wala Quwata Illa Billah" is a treasure from the treasures of Jannah?

So keep on saying it, and keep on getting rich in good deeds.

Healthy habit

Whenever you hear the athan, do the following:
1. Repeat after the mu'athin.
2. Say the du'aa of the athan when the athan is over.

CHAPTER REVIEW

ACTIVITY TIME

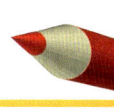

Listen to the athan on a tape. Then, the say athan and iqamah to your teacher and parents.

Study questions

1. What is the purpose of the athan?
2. What is the purpose of the iqamah?
3. Say the athan and iqamah, and tell the difference between them.
4. What should you do when you hear the athan?
5. Say the du'aa we should practice after the athan.

UNIT C CHAPTER 8

I Fast in Ramadan

questions?

1. When do Muslims fast?
2. How important is fasting?
3. What is the Arabic word for fasting?

word watch

Ramadan	رمضان
sawm	صَوْم
Iftar	إفطار
suhoor	سُحور
Fajr	فَجر
Ar-Rayyan	الرَّيان
Salat Al-Taraweeh	صلاة التراويح
niyyah	نِيَّة

WORDS OF WISDOM
HOLY QUR'AN

سورة البقرة
Surat Al-Baqarah: ayah 185

بِسْمِ اللَّهِ الرَّحْمَٰنِ الرَّحِيمِ

﴿ شَهْرُ رَمَضَانَ الَّذِي أُنزِلَ فِيهِ الْقُرْآنُ هُدًى لِّلنَّاسِ وَبَيِّنَاتٍ مِّنَ الْهُدَىٰ وَالْفُرْقَانِ ۚ فَمَن شَهِدَ مِنكُمُ الشَّهْرَ فَلْيَصُمْهُ ۖ وَمَن كَانَ مَرِيضًا أَوْ عَلَىٰ سَفَرٍ فَعِدَّةٌ مِّنْ أَيَّامٍ أُخَرَ ۗ يُرِيدُ اللَّهُ بِكُمُ الْيُسْرَ وَلَا يُرِيدُ بِكُمُ الْعُسْرَ وَلِتُكْمِلُوا الْعِدَّةَ وَلِتُكَبِّرُوا اللَّهَ عَلَىٰ مَا هَدَاكُمْ وَلَعَلَّكُمْ تَشْكُرُونَ ۝١٨٥ ﴾

TRANSLITERATION

[185] Shahru ramadan-allathee onzila feeh-il-qur'anu hudal linnasi wabayyinatim-min-alhuda walfurqan, faman shahida minkum-ush-shahra falyasumh, waman kana mareedan aw ala safarin fa'iddatum-min ayyamin ukhar, yureed-ullahu bikum-ul-ysra wala yureedu bikum-ul-usr wa litukmilol iddata walitukabbiro-llaha ala ma hadakum wala'allakum tashkuroon.

TRANSLATION

[185] Ramadan is the (month) in which was sent down the Qur'an, as a guide to mankind, also clear (signs) for guidance and judgment (between right and wrong). So everyone of you who is present (at his home) during that month should spend it in fasting, but if anyone is ill, or on a journey, the prescribed period (should be made up) by days later. God intends every facility for you; He does not want to put you to difficulties. (He wants you) to complete the prescribed period, and to glorify Him in that He has guided you; and perchance you shall be grateful.

Zaid went to his classroom one early morning. It was the first day of **Ramadan** رَمضان, and he was fasting. When he got inside the classroom, he saw a new student whose name was Ahmed.

Zaid: Assalamu Alaykum. Ramadan Mubarak. My name is Zaid.

Ahmed: Oh, to you, too. I'm Ahmed. I'm new here.

Zaid: Welcome. How does it feel to fast?

Ahmed: Well, actually, I'm not fasting!

Zaid: Why? Didn't you eat suhoor سُحور ?

Ahmed: Suhoor? What is that?

Zaid: **Suhoor** is the meal that Muslims eat before **Fajr** فَجر time. It helps us fast the whole day.

Ahmed: Well, I'm not used to it, and I have to eat my lunch.

Zaid: Do you know that fasting, or **sawm** صوم , is one of the five pillars of Islam?

Ahmed: Really?

Zaid: Yes. If we do not fast in Ramadan, Allah سبحانه وتعالى will not be pleased with us.

Ahmed: Can you tell me how we fast?

Zaid: Fasting means not eating or drinking from dawn until sunset. After sunset, we eat Iftar إفطار .

Ahmed: What is Iftar?

Zaid: **Iftar** is the meal that we eat to break our fast. When we break our fast, we say a special du'aa:

GREAT DU'AA

اللّهُمَّ لَكَ صُمْتُ وبِكَ آمَنْتُ وَعلى رِزقِكَ أفْطرْتُ

"Allahuma laka sumtu wa bika amantu wa ala rizqika aftart."

"O Allah, I have fasted for You, I believed in You, and with Your gifts I break my fast."

C71

Ahmed: Are there other things we should do in Ramadan?

Zaid: Yes. Every night, people go to the masjid and pray Salat Al-Taraweeh صلاة التراويح after 'Isha prayer.

Ahmed: Wow! Muslims do many things in Ramadan. Is it because it's the month of fasting?

Zaid: Not only that. The Holy Qur'an was revealed during the month of Ramadan to Prophet Muhammad ﷺ. Also, shayateen are locked up during the month of Ramadan. It's a very special month.

Ahmed: Really? I didn't know that.

Zaid: One more thing. Allah سبحانه وتعالى promised a special gate to enter Jannah for only those who fast. It's called the **Ar-Rayyan** الرَّيّان Gate.

Ahmed: Don't you feel hungry and thirsty when you fast?

Zaid: Yes, of course. Allah wants us to build strong bodies that can stand hunger. He also wants us to feel how poor and hungry people feel, so we will help them.

Ahmed: It must be so hard to fast all day long!

Zaid: Not really. You feel hungry the most on the first day, but it becomes easier because your body gets used to it.

Ahmed: Thank you so much, Zaid, for telling me all this about Ramadan. I will start fasting tomorrow so I can please Allah and get lots of hasanat.

Zaid: Insha'Allah. Uh oh, class is starting.

Ahmed: See you tonight at Salat Al-Taraweeh!

Teacher Hibah: Assalamu Alaykum and Ramadan Mubarak, children! We are now in a very special month. Today we have a new student. His name is Ahmed. Welcome, Ahmed! Why don't you all greet each other?
Zaid walked up to Ahmed.
Class: Assalamu Alaykum, Ahmed.
Ahmed: Wa Alaykum Assalam, Everyone. Thank you.
Teacher Hibah: Okay, class. Let's start today's lesson.
Mona: Teacher, I have a question about fasting.
Teacher Hibah: Go ahead, Mona.
Mona: This morning, I forgot that I was fasting. I went to the kitchen and drank my milk. Did I break my fast?
Teacher Hibah: Then Allah has sent you a present! You made your **niyyah** to fast, then you forgot that you were fasting. Allah will forgive you.
Mona: So my fast will still count?
Teacher Hibah: Yes, insha'Allah!

Oops!

Ahmed: Wow, even if you eat your whole lunch?
Everyone started laughing.
Teacher Hibah smiled and said: Yes, but you must truly forget that you were fasting.
Bilal: Alhamdulillah, Allah is so kind.

Mona: What breaks our fast? How do we know when it won't count?

Teacher Hibah: If you eat or drink, even though you know you are fasting, you will break your fast. However, if you are sick, you don't have to fast, but you will have to make it up.

Zaid: What should we do to make up for days we miss?

Teacher Hibah: You make them up by fasting other days after Ramadan.

Ahmed: This school is great. It teaches me things about my religion. Thank you, Teacher.

Teacher Hibah: You're welcome, Ahmed.

Nasheed

RAMADAN

In blessed Ramadan
A Muslim fasts for thirty days.
In blessed Ramadan
To Allah we give thanks and praise.
In blessed Ramadan.

In blessed Ramadan
We wake and eat before the dawn.
In blessed Ramadan
We eat suhoor; the day is long.
In blessed Ramadan.

In blessed Ramadan
We fast until the sun goes down.
In blessed Ramadan,
Our families all will gather around.
In blessed Ramadan.

In blessed Ramadan
We savor each delicious bite.
In blessed Ramadan

We pray together every night.
In blessed Ramadan.

In blessed Ramadan
The fast is done and Eid is here.
In blessed Ramadan.

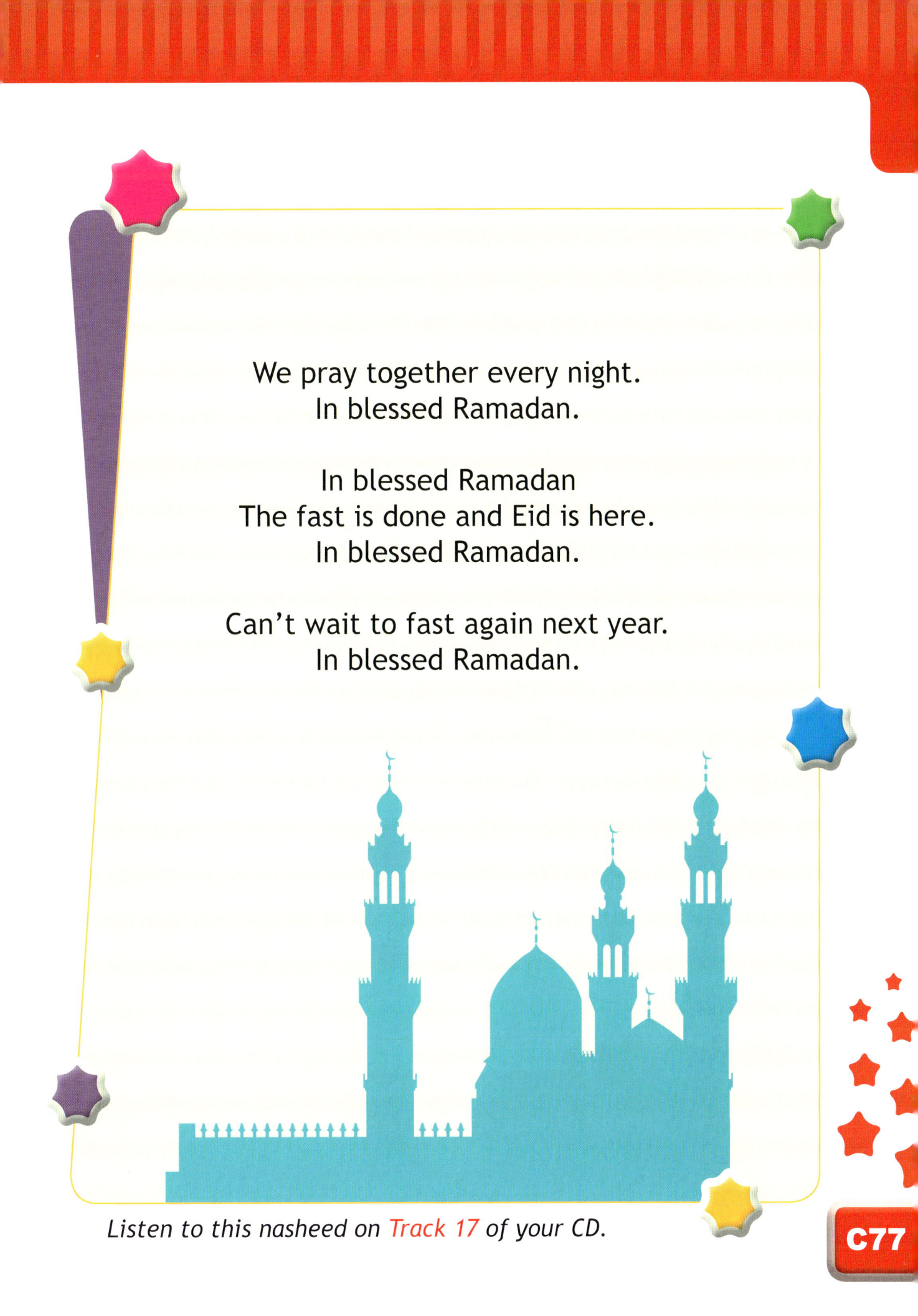

Can't wait to fast again next year.
In blessed Ramadan.

Listen to this nasheed on *Track 17* of your CD.

WORDS OF WISDOM
HADEETH SHAREEF

حديث شريف

Narrated by Muslim & Bukhari

عن أبي هريرة رضي الله عنه: قال رسول الله ﷺ:
"من صام رمضان إيمانا واحتسابا غفر الله له ما تَقَدَّم مِنْ ذَنْبِهِ" رواه البخاري ومسلم

TRANSLITERATION

"Man sama Ramadan imanan wahtisaman ghafaar Allahu lahu ma taqaddama min thanbih."

TRANSLATION

Abu Hurayrah رضي الله عنه reported that the Prophet ﷺ said: "He who fasts Ramadan out of faith and to gain reward, God will forgive all of his past sins."

Healthy habit

When we fast during Ramadan, it makes us feel how the needy people feel. Try to fast the whole month of Ramadan, if you can.

Healthy habit

Giving Charity
Save some of your money to share with the needy. Give it to the poor around Eid time! Our beloved Prophet Muhammad ﷺ was the most generous during the month of Ramadan.

CHAPTER REVIEW

ACTIVITY TIME

Ask your parents how they felt when they fasted during the month of Ramadan at your age.

Study questions

1. What is the name of the month during which Muslims fast?
2. What is the Arabic word for fasting?
3. When do we start and end our day of fasting?
4. What is suhoor? When do we eat the meal of suhoor?
5. What is the meal that we eat at sunset called?
6. Allah will invite Muslims who fast Ramadan to enter Jannah from a special gate. What is the name of that gate?

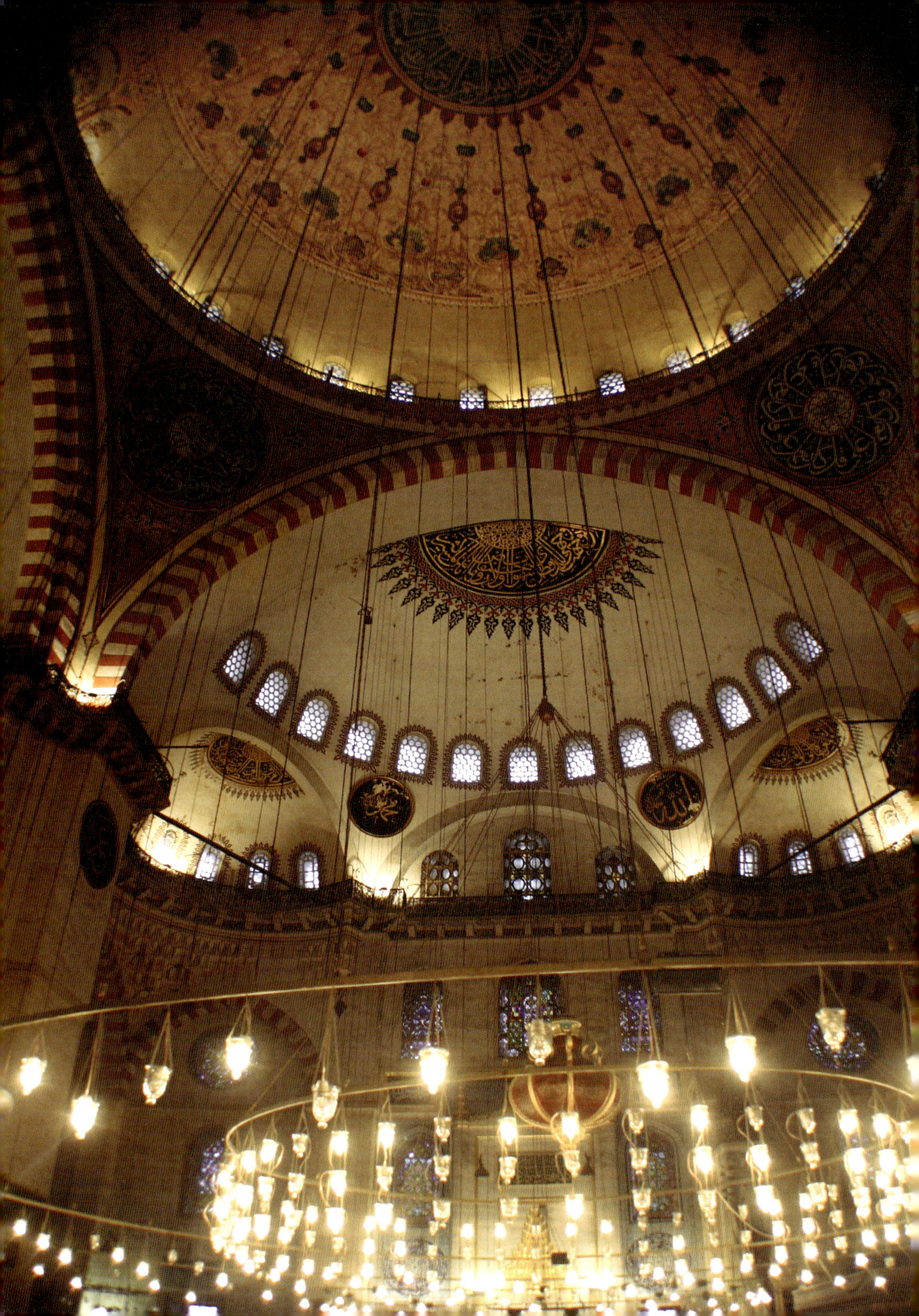

UNIT D

ISLAM IN THE WORLD

Chapter 1	It Is Eid! Allahu Akbar! D2
Chapter 2	Eid Around the World D8
Chapter 3	Masajid Around the World D20

UNIT D CHAPTER 1

It Is Eid! Allahu Akbar!

questions?

1. Do you love Eid?
2. How many Eids do Muslims celebrate?
3. What things do you do on Eid?

word watch

Eid al-Fitr عيد الفطر
Eid al-Adha عيد الأضحى
Salat Al-Eid صلاة العيد
khutbah خُطْبة
Eid Mubarak عيد مُبارك

People everywhere have special days. People celebrate many different things. They celebrate seasons of the year. They celebrate births and weddings. They celebrate important events and people. They celebrate Allah in their own ways. On special days, people join together to celebrate. They stop working and have fun together. They visit each other and share special foods. They wear their best clothes.

Muslims have special days, too. All Muslims celebrate twice each year. A day of celebration in Arabic is called Eid. Muslims everywhere celebrate Eid. The Qur'an and Prophet Muhammad's Sunnah teach Muslims about Eid.

The first Eid is called **Eid al-Fitr** عيد الفطر which comes after the month of Ramadan. We celebrate the end of fasting during Eid al-Fitr for three days.

The second Eid is called **Eid al-Adha** عيد الأضحى , which comes during the month of Hajj, Thu-al-Hijjah. Muslims celebrate this Eid for four days. In Eid al-Adha, people slaughter a sheep or a goat to remember Prophet Ibraheem and his son Isma'eel. They share the meat with family, friends, and poor people.

Before Eid, people clean their homes. They make sweets and cook special food for Eid.

Everyone celebrates by wearing nice clothes. Many children get new colorful clothes and shoes.

Families go to the Eid prayer, which is called Salat Al-Eid صلاة العيد . The prayer is held outdoors, in a community center, or in the masjid. All the Muslims pray to Allah. They listen quietly to the imam's khutbah خُطبة or speech.

After Eid prayer, the Muslims greet each other. Children get gifts, candy, balloons and money. Friends, family, and neighbors visit each other. They eat delicious food together. They also give food and money to poor people.

A Day of Eid
With Leena and Zaid's Family

Leena: Baba, when will we know if Eid al-Fitr is tomorrow?

Baba: When the hilal, or crescent moon, is sighted.

Leena: What does the crescent moon have to do with Eid, Baba?

Baba: When we see the moon, it means Ramadan is over and the month of Shawwal has begun. The first three days of Shawwal are the days of Eid al-Fitr.

Zaid: Oh, that is so cool!

Baba: If we don't see the moon, that means we are going to fast for one more day. Then after that it will be Eid!

Leena: I can't wait until Eid! I hope it's tomorrow.

Leena and Zaid stayed up with their parents at night to wait for the news of Eid. They called the masjid, and they found out that Eid would be the next day. Leena and Zaid were very excited.
The next morning, they woke up and everyone in the family was saying "Eid Mubarak" عيد مُبارك to each other. They were all very happy that it was Eid.
The children put on their new clothes, and the family went to pray Salat Al-Eid together at the masjid.

D5

Leena: Masha'Allah, there are so many Muslims praying Eid prayer today.
Baba: Eid is a very special celebration for all Muslims.

The family prayed Salat Al-Eid and then listened to the khutbah. After the prayer, the family went to visit relatives and friends. When they got home, the children were surprised with many presents from their parents. They were very happy and excited.
After opening their presents, they ate a very special dinner together as one big happy family.

CHAPTER REVIEW

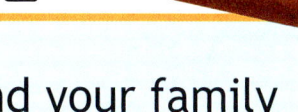

ACTIVITY TIME

Write a paragraph on how you and your family celebrate Eid.

Healthy habit

Always go with your family to Salat Al-Eid. Make sure to offer the prayer there and not miss it.

Study questions

1. What two holidays do Muslims celebrate?

2. After what month does Eid al-Fitr come?

3. In which month does Eid al-Fitr happen? How about Eid al-Adha?

4. Who are we remembering when we slaughter a sheep or goat in Eid al-Adha?

5. Describe what happens on Eid day.

UNIT D CHAPTER 2

Eid Around the World*

questions?

1. Do Muslims celebrate Eid in different ways around the world?
2. How do Muslims in your country celebrate Eid?

word watch

Pakistan	باكستان
Iran	إيران
Egypt	مصر
Turkey	تركيا
Trinidad	ترينداد
Malaysia	ماليزيا
China	الصين
Gambia	غامبيا

* Adapted from Suzan Douglass' (1995) Eid Mubarak! Islamic Celebration Around the World.

D8

EID AROUND THE WORLD

You have read about how Muslims celebrate Eid. Now, you will read about special ways to celebrate Eid. Muslims live all over the world. Muslims in each country have different customs. They have fun in different ways. There are around a billion and a half Muslims in the world. Muslims live on all the continents.

PAKISTAN

Pakistan باكستان is a Muslim country in Asia. Islamabad is the capital city of Pakistan. Karachi, Lahore, and Peshawar are the names of other big cities in Pakistan. Pakistan has very high mountains. The stars sparkle at night. The sky is clear in the mountains.

In Pakistan, at the end of Ramadan, families watch for the new moon. They watch from the tops of their houses. Street singers go through the streets. People hug each other. The children like to stay up late. They help to get ready for Eid. On the day of Eid, people wear fancy clothes. Women and girls paint henna on their hands and feet. Children get money and gifts. They enjoy swings and rides.

Leepa Valley, Pakistan

IRAN

Iran إيـران is a Muslim country in Asia. Tehran is the capital city of Iran. Masajid are beautiful in Iran. It is the night before Eid. The children have shiny, new shoes. The children are very excited. They put the new shoes under their pillows on this night. They dream about Eid the next day.

Amirkabir Dam, Iran

D11

EGYPT

Muhammed Ali Basha mosque in Cairo, Egypt

Egypt مصر is a Muslim country in Africa. Cairo is the capital city of Egypt. It is called the city of 1000 minarets because Cairo has more than a thousand minarets. The world's longest river, the Nile, is in Egypt. It is more than 4000 miles long. Egypt has huge and famous pyramids. They were built more than 3000 years ago. More than 80 million people live in Egypt. In Ramadan, children get colored lanterns and have a parade. They hold the lanterns high. They sing songs. Neighbors give them gifts.

On Eid, colored lights decorate houses and shops. Children wear brightly colored clothes. Families go to parks and they play and eat together. They ride horses and swings, laugh and have fun. Everyone enjoys Eid.

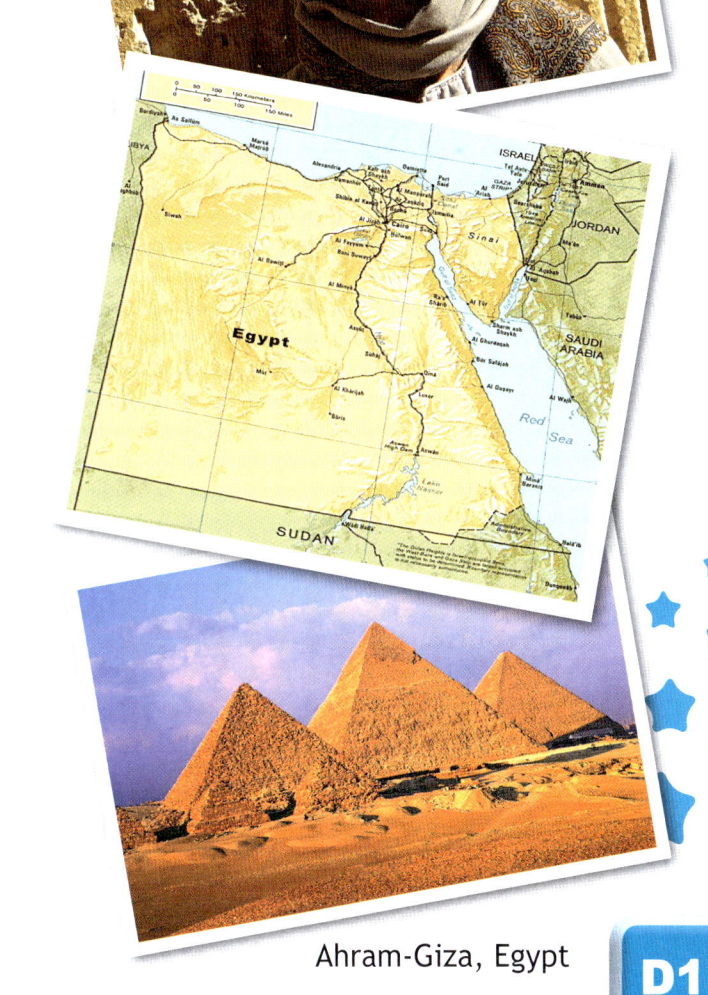

Ahram-Giza, Egypt

D13

TRINIDAD

Trinidad is a country in North America, in the Carribean Sea. Trinidad is a beautiful island. Port of Spain is the capital city of Trinidad. Muslims came to Trinidad a long time ago. Their ancestors came from Africa and India. Many Muslims live in Trinidad. There are more than 100 masajid in the country. Christians and Hindus live there too. On Eid, Muslims have the day off. Schools and offices close. Muslim families celebrate Eid. They go to prayer. They buy sweets. They visit each other's homes. Christians and Hindus come to visit, too. Muslims send sweets to neighbors. The television stations show Islamic programs all day.

MALAYSIA

Malaysia ماليزيا is a Muslim country in Asia. Part of Malaysia is on a peninsula. A peninsula has water on three sides.
Another part of Malaysia is on an island. An island is surrounded by water. Kuala Lampur is the capital city of Malaysia. Formely the tallest buildings in the world, the Petronas Tower 1 and the Petronas Tower 2 have 88 floors and are 452 meters tall. Malaysia is a warm, rainy country. Rice, bamboo, and coconuts grow there. On the day before Eid, families cook special rice. They mix the rice with coconut milk then stuff it inside hollow bamboo stalks. They hang the bamboo over a big fire and the rice cooks all day. The children play and laugh. They like the big fire.

CHINA

China الصين is in Asia.
China is a very large country.
Beijing is the capital city of China.
Hong Kong, Shanghai, and Canton are other big cities in China. More than a billion people live in China.
More than 60 million of them are Muslims. Chinese Muslims share special bread on Eid. They make dough from flour, then fry the dough in hot oil. Chinese Muslims know a story about the bread.
A poor woman once made bread for Prophet Muhammad ﷺ. She had only a little flour and oil. The Prophet tasted the woman's bread. It tasted very good because she had made the bread with love. Prophet Muhammad thanked and blessed her.

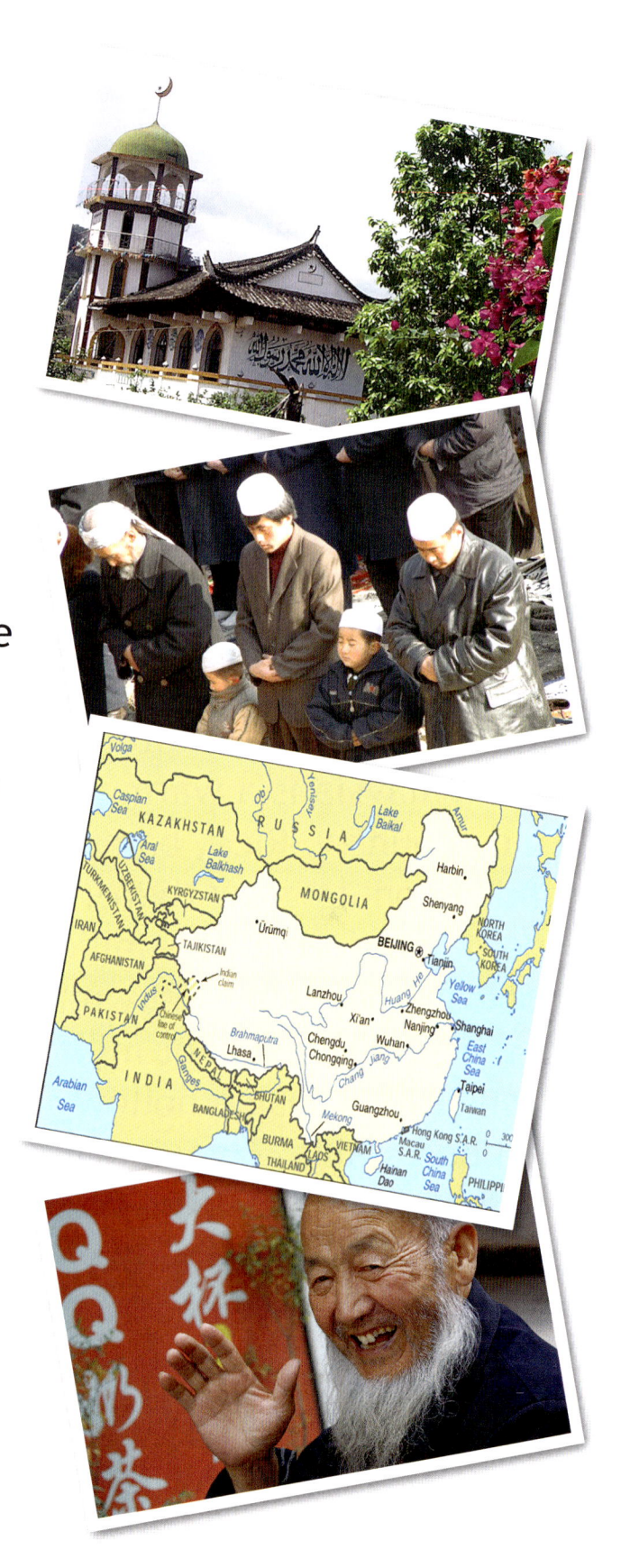

GAMBIA

Gambia غامبيا is a Muslim country in West Africa. It is near the North Atlantic Ocean. Banjul is the capital city. Families live together in groups. They share water from a well. They plant fruit trees.

For Eid Al-Adha, the families buy sheep. The children are very happy. They bring grass and water for the sheep. Children help their fathers sacrifice the sheep. They cut the meat and give some to other families. Each child takes some to neighbors.

In each house, families cook pots full of food. Women carry the pots on their heads. They put the pots under a big tree. Everyone wears new clothes. Everyone brings a chair and a spoon, and the whole family shares the food.

TURKEY

Turkey تركيا is a Muslim country between Europe and Asia. Turkey has mountains and coasts. It has farms and big cities. Ankara is the capital city of Turkey. Istanbul is another big city in Turkey.

In Ramadan, Muslims eat a meal before dawn. It is still dark outside. A drummer walks through the streets. Sleeping people hear his drum. Boom-ba-ba-boom! Boom-ba-ba-boom! Wake up to eat! Wake up to pray! On Eid, the drummer comes again. People give him sweets and money.

CHAPTER REVIEW

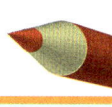

ACTIVITY TIME

People celebrate Eid differently around the world. Choose a country and collect pictures that show how Muslims celebrate Eid there. Post those pictures on a board and talk about it to your class.

Study questions

1. What do women and girls do in Pakistan for Eid?
2. What does the drummer do in Turkey?
3. In Malaysia, what special food do they cook for Eid?
4. Why do Chinese Muslims make bread during Eid?
5. In Gambia, what do the families buy for Eid ul Adha?

D19

UNIT D CHAPTER 3

Masajid Around the World

questions?

1. Do you go to the masjid often?
2. What is the most beautiful masjid you have ever seen?
3. What are some different things you can find in a masjid?

word watch

مسجد	masjid
مساجد	masajid
مِحْراب	mihrab
مِنبر	minbar
مِئذنة	mi'thanah
منارة	manarah
قُبَّة	qubbah
مُصَلّى	musalla

A **masjid** is a place of worship and remembrance of Allah. We worship Allah in the masjid. **Masajid** means more than one masjid. We call the masajid around the world the houses of Allah.

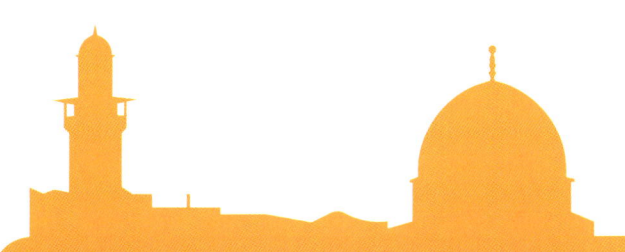

ALL MASAJID AROUND THE WORLD ARE HOUSES OF ALLAH!

Do you know that the word "masjid" comes from "sujood," which you do during prayer to Allah?

Let's make a list of things that all masajid have in common.

1. A masjid has a mihrab. A **mihrab** is the place where the imam stands and leads Muslims in the prayer.

2. A masjid has a minbar. A **minbar** is the place where the imam stands to deliver his khutbah.

3. Masajid have at least one long tower, which is called a **mi'thanah** or **manarah**, or minaret. In many Muslim countries, the athan is called from the top of the minaret.

4. Every masjid has an area for wudoo', where people clean themselves for prayer.

5. The biggest part of the masjid is the prayer hall, or **musalla**. People there stand in lines behind the imam. Inside the prayer hall, you find bookracks with copies of the Qur'ans on them.

6. Many masajid also have beautiful domes. A dome is called **qubbah** in Arabic.

Du'aa for entering the masjid:

When we enter any masjid, we should say:

بسم الله. اللهم افتح لي أبواب رحمتك

Bismillah, Allahumma iftah lee abwaba rahmatik
"Bismillah, O Allah open Your doors of mercy for me."

Du'aa of leaving the masjid:

And when we leave the masjid we should say:

اللهم إني أسألك من فضلك

Allahumma inni as alok min fadlik
"O Allah, provide for me from Your bounties"

THE WORLD IS FULL OF BEAUTIFUL MASAJID!

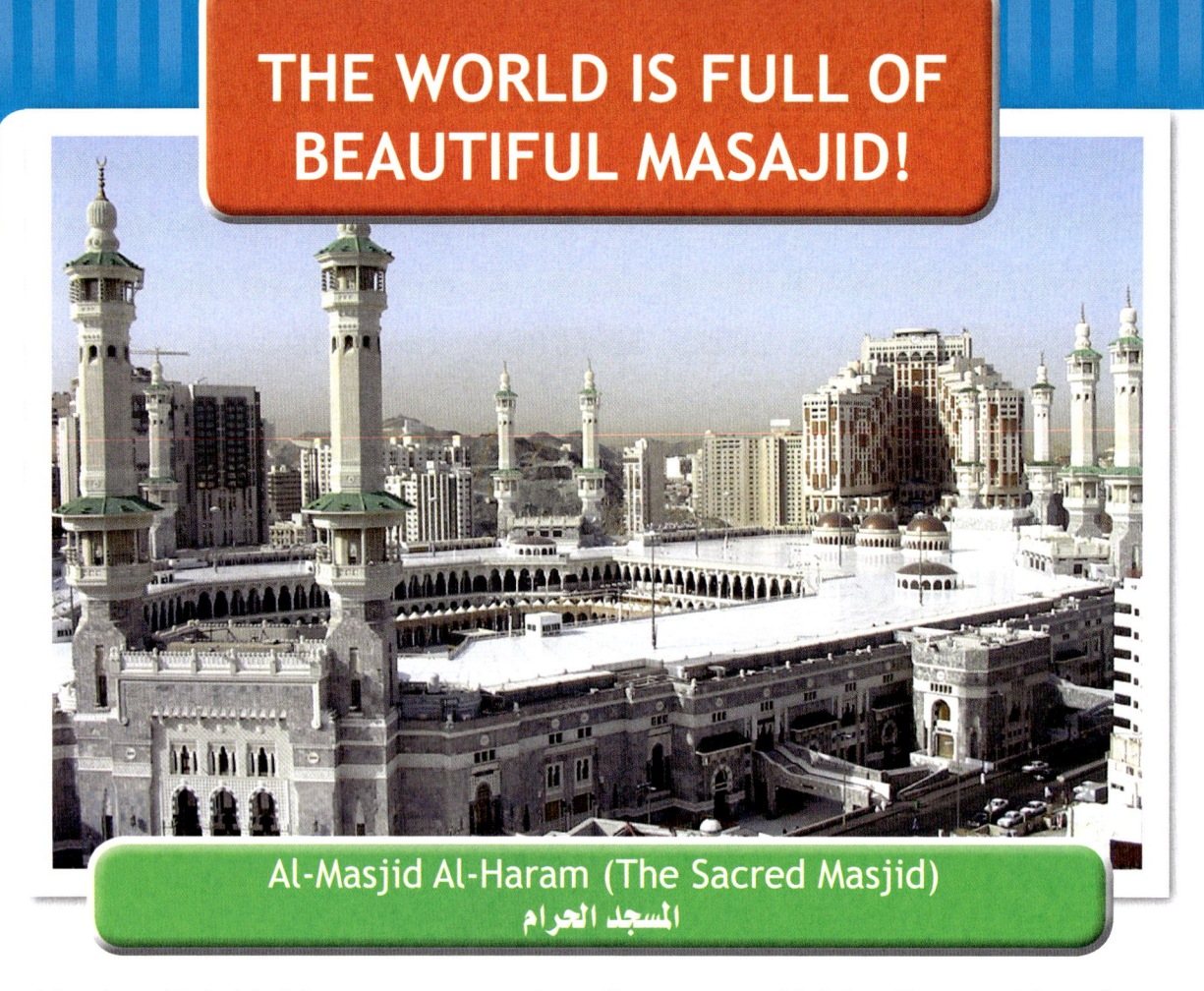

Al-Masjid Al-Haram (The Sacred Masjid)
المسجد الحرام

Al-Masjid Al-Haram was the first masjid built on Earth. It was built by Prophet Ibraheem.

Al-Ka'bah is in the center of this masjid.
It has nine beautiful and very tall mi'thanah, or minarets.

Praying one prayer in Al-Masjid Al-Haram gives us the reward of 100,000 prayers elsewhere!

The masjid is located in the city of Makkah in Saudi Arabia.

This is the holiest masjid on Earth, and it is the largest masjid, too.

Al-Masjid Al-Nabawi (The Prophet's Masjid)
المسجد النبوي

Al-Masjid Al-Nabawi is the Prophet's Masjid.

It is located in the city of Madinah, also in Saudi Arabia.

Prophet Muhammad ﷺ and the sahabah built this masjid in Madinah.

This is the place where the Prophet ﷺ is buried.

Praying one prayer in Al-Masjid Al-Nabawi gives us the reward of 1000 prayers elsewhere!

Al-Masjid Al-Aqsa (The Farthest Masjid)
المسجد الأقصى

This masjid is located in the city of Jerusalem, in Palestine. Prophet Muhammad ﷺ started his journey of Al-Mi'raj to the seventh heaven from Al-Masjid Al-Aqsa.

Praying in Al-Masjid Al-Aqsa gives us the reward of 500 prayers!

The Masjid of Sultan Ahmad
المسجد السلطان أحمد

The Ottomans built this masjid in the city of Istanbul in Turkey.

It has six minarets, and many beautiful domes.

This masjid is the largest in Turkey, and one of the largest masajid around the world.

It is also called the Blue Mosque because it has blue tiles and paint inside.

Al-Jami' Al-Azhar
المسجد الأزهر

Al-Jami' Al-Azhar is located in Cairo, Egypt. It was built in the year 969, more than a thousand years ago.

It became a very popular place of worshipping and learning.

Thousands of scholars and imams have studied at the Islamic University of Al-Azhar.

Faisal Masjid
مسجد فيصل

The Faisal Masjid is located in the city of Islamabad in Pakistan. It has four very high minarets, and was completed in 1986. The masjid is the largest in Pakistan and includes an Islamic university.

Jama Masjid
المسجد الجامع

This masjid was built in 1650 in Delhi, India.

Mughal Emperor Shah Jehan built it.

He is the same emperor who built the Taj Mahal.

The masjid is made out of red stones and marble, and it has a very big courtyard where people pray.

It is the largest masjid in India. It is also one of the oldest masajid there.

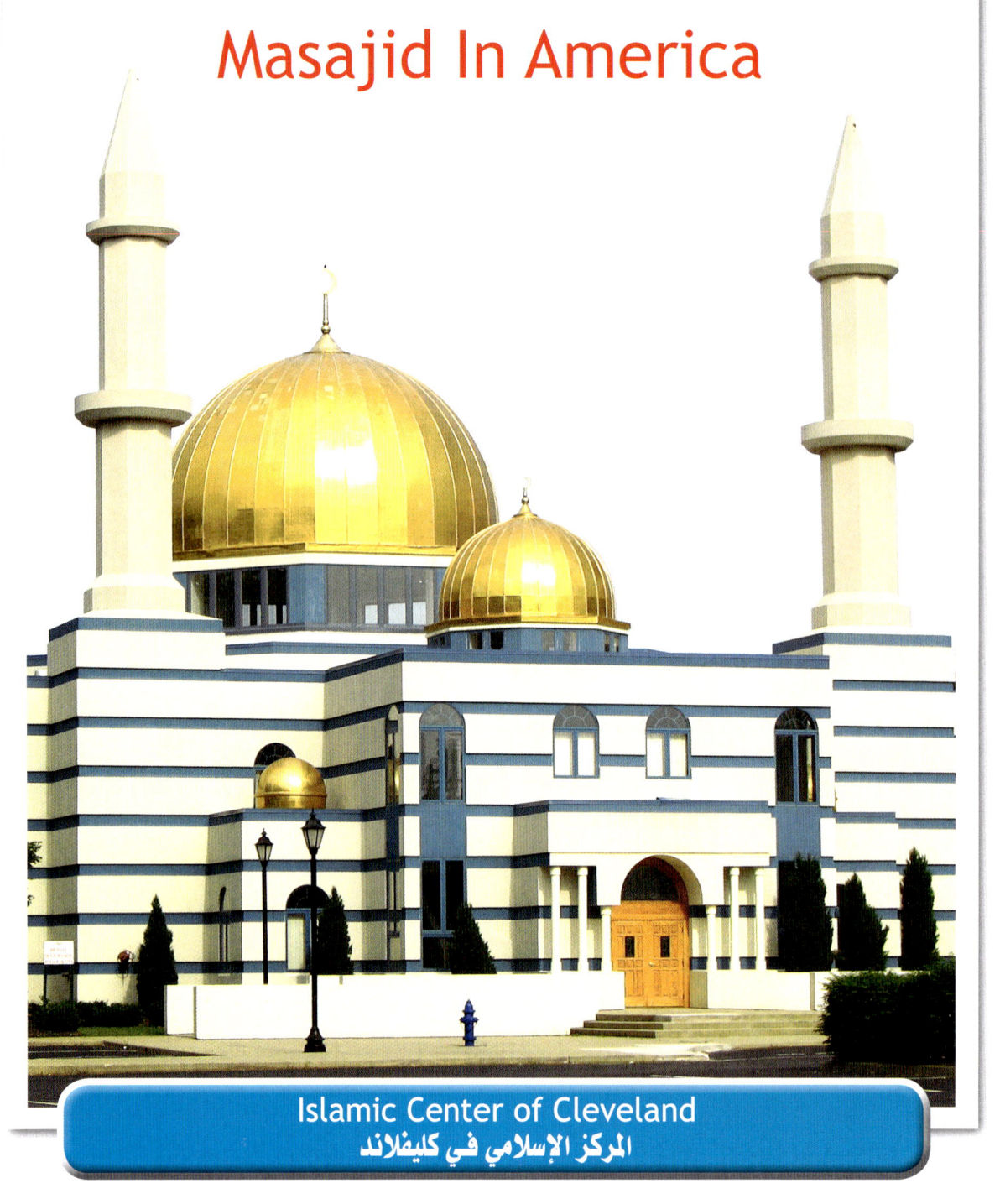

Masajid In America

Islamic Center of Cleveland
المركز الإسلامي في كليفلاند

The Islamic center of Cleveland is one of the most beautiful masajid in the United States. It is located in Cleveland, Ohio. The outside of the masjid has blue stripes with a gold dome.

Omar Ibn Khattab Masjid
مسجد عمر بن الخطاب

This masjid was named after the great Khaleefah Omar Ibn Al-Khattab. The masjid is located in Los Angeles, California. An old lady gave money to start building the masjid in 1977. It took 15 years for the masjid to be built.

In Ramadan of 1993, the masjid was finally completed. Today, there are many Muslims in Los Angeles.

Mother of Mosques in America

Mother of Mosques is located in Cedar Rapids, Iowa. It was built in 1935. It is a very simple masjid, but it is very special because it is the oldest masjid still in use in America.

D33

Healthy habit

Always visit the masajid in your area and wherever you go. They are the best places that you can ever be.

WORDS OF WISDOM
HADEETH SHAREEF

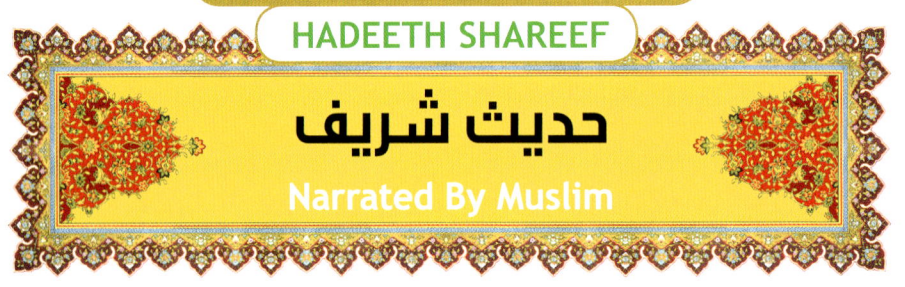

حديث شريف

Narrated By Muslim

عن أبي هريرة رضي الله عنه: قال رسول الله ﷺ:
"أحَبُّ البِلادِ إلى اللهِ مساجِدُها." رواه مسلم

TRANSLITERATION
"Ahabb-ul-biladi illa Allah masajidaha."

TRANSLATION
"The most beloved places to God on Earth are the mosques."

CHAPTER REVIEW

ACTIVITY TIME

1. Find a picture of a masjid. Label the minaret and the dome.

2. Draw a masjid from your imagination that has a dome and a minaret.

Study questions

1. Name some parts of a masjid.

2. Where is Al-Masjid Al-Haram?

3. Which of the masajid is in Istanbul, Turkey?

4. What du'aa should you say when you enter and exit any masjid?

5. Name five of the great masajid around the world.

6. Say a Hadeeth on the importance of the masjid.

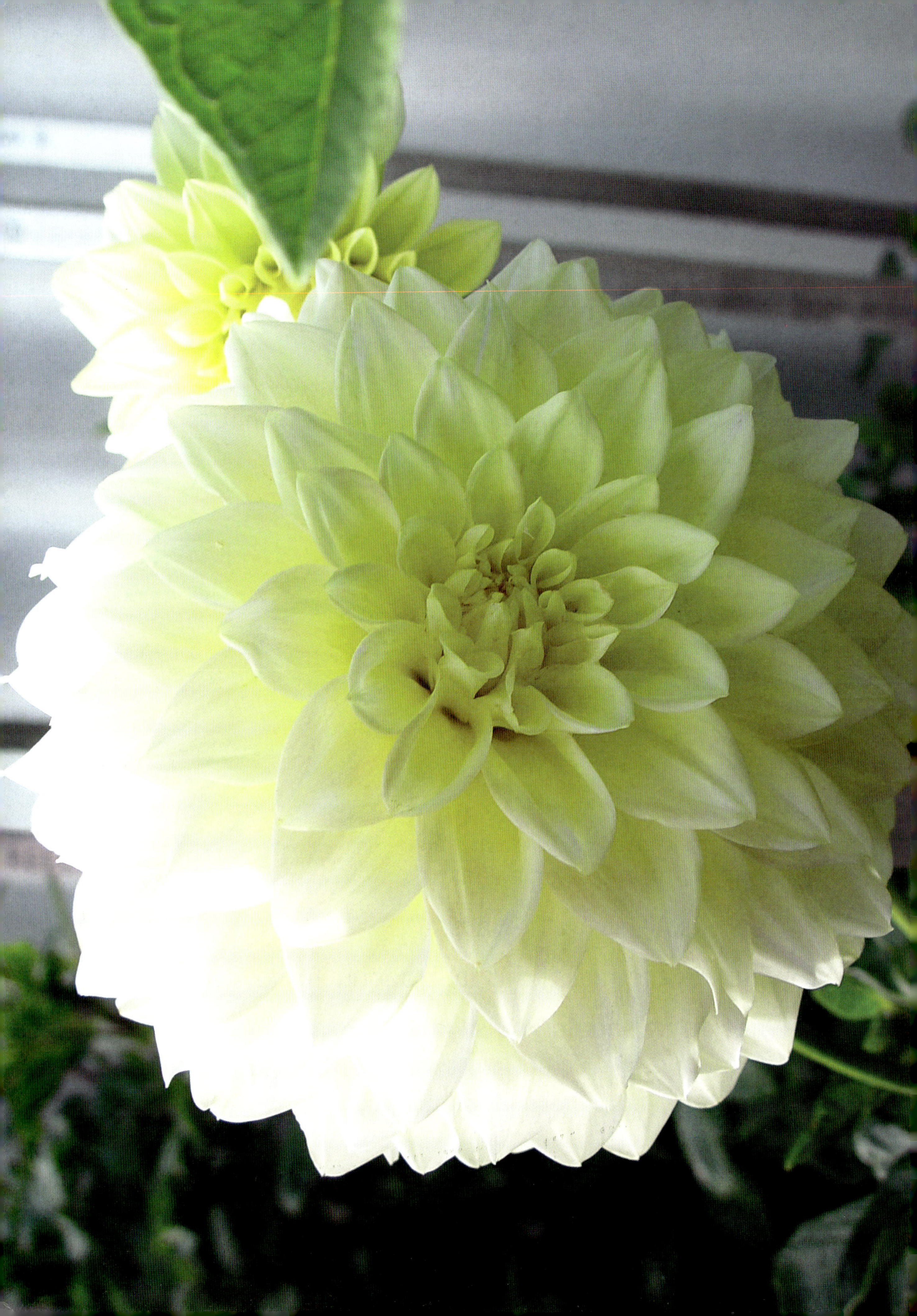

UNIT E

MY MUSLIM MANNERS

Chapter 1	Who Is My Role Model?	E2
Chapter 2	I Am a Muslim; I Am Honest	E12
Chapter 3	I Love My Family	E20
Chapter 4	I Respect My Teachers and Elders	E30
Chapter 5	Zaid and Leena Go to the Masjid	E40
Chapter 6	Learning Is First	E50
Chapter 7	My Muslim Room	E60

UNIT E CHAPTER 1

Who Is My Role Model?

questions?

1. Who is your role model?
2. How do role models behave?
3. Would you like to be a role model to others?

word watch

[qudwah قُدْوة]

WHAT IS A ROLE MODEL?

Qudwah قُدْوة is the word for role model in Arabic.

A qudwah is:
- Someone who makes you think of doing good things.
- Someone whom you respect--you would like to follow and want to be like him or her.
- Someone who has taught you great things.
- Someone who pleases Allah and encourages you to do the same.

Let's listen to some boys and girls who have role models in their lives:

مُحَمَّد ﷺ

My role model is Prophet Muhammad ﷺ.
He taught me how to do and say great things.
He stood up strongly for what he believed in.
He had a hard time with nonbelievers, but he never gave up.
He taught me how to be honest, strong, kind, fair, and helpful to others.
He made bad people become good.
Prophet Muhammad ﷺ is my role model, qudwah.

أبو بكر الصديق

My role model is Abu Bakr As-Siddeeq, the first Muslim khaleefah.
He was Prophet Muhammad's best friend.
He taught me how to have a kind heart and to treat people with kindness.
He spoke only when it was important.
From him, I learned how to think before I speak.
He was a great doer; he worked much more than he talked.
I learned from him how to be a good friend. He was a great friend to the Prophet ﷺ.
Abu Bakr was a great friend and a great teacher.
Abu Bakr is my role model.

Khadeejah Bintu Khuwayled خديجة بنت خويلد

My role model is Khadeejah Bintu Khuwayled, the first wife of Prophet Muhammad ﷺ. She and the Prophet ﷺ had four great daughters. They are Zaynab, Ruqayyah, Ummu Kulthoom and Fatimah. She taught me how to work hard for Islam. She taught me how to support Muslims. She used her money for the sake of Allah to help Muslims. She was the first person to believe in the Prophet ﷺ and become a Muslim. Khadeejah was a great wife. Khadeejah is my role model.

أمي My Mother

My mother is my role model.
She is someone I can always count on.
She is someone who gives me courage and love.
She is always there when I'm healthy or sick, or when I'm happy or sad.
She always believes in me and tells me I can do things.
She cooks my food, cleans my clothes, and wipes my tears when I am sad.
She forgives me when I make mistakes.
Sometimes she punishes me, but this teaches me not to do something bad again.
She is my best friend.
I ask Allah to grant my mother Paradise.
She and Dad have given me a great life on Earth.
She is a great mother.
She is my role model.

My Father   أبي

My role model is my father.
He works hard every day.
He puts food on our table and a roof over our heads.
He taught me how to pray.
He taught me how to ride a bike.
He taught me how to swim.
He taught me to be kind.
He tells me stories of the prophets.
He wants me to be even better than he is.
He always makes me happy.
He is happy even with the small good things I do, and he tells me he is proud of me.
He taught me how to work hard and to never give up.
My father is my friend.
When I grow up, I want to be just like him.
May Allah keep him safe.
He is a great father.
He is my role model.

My Teacher معلمتي

My teacher is my role model.
She teaches me to seek knowledge, and to be among the stars.
When I tell her "I can't do it," she does not accept that.
Instead, she always tells me to say "Insha'Allah, I will try my best."
She taught me to be confident in myself.
She taught me how to work hard so I could reach my goals.
She listens to me when I talk.
She gives me time, and she thinks I'm special.
She tells me and the other students that "Allah wants you to be the best, and the best never rest."
She always gives me courage.
She taught me the real meaning of achievement.
May Allah reward her and bless her.
She is my teacher.
She is my role model.

Abdullah ibn Mas'oud عبدالله ابن مسعود

My role model is Abdullah ibn Mas'oud.
He was a great sahabi of the Prophet ﷺ.
He was a great reader of the Holy Qur'an.
He was the first to recite Al-Qur'an aloud by Al-Ka'bah. The non-believers beat him for that, but he was patient.
He learned 70 surahs of Al-Qur'an directly from the Prophet ﷺ.
The Prophet ﷺ used to love listening to Abdullah ibn Mas'oud reading the Qur'an.
Abdullah ibn Mas'oud learned the Qur'an, memorized it, and taught it to others.
Abdullah loved the Qur'an, and he tried to do everything it said.
He has encouraged me to learn Al-Qur'an and memorize it.
He was a great sahabi.
He is my role model.

Hakeem حكيم

My role model is Hakeem Olajuwon. He is from Nigeria, a Muslim country in Africa. He was a great basketball player. He won two NBA championships with his team, the Houston Rockets. He is also a good Muslim. He prays, fasts, gives zakah and makes Hajj. He has great Muslim manners. When his team won the championship, they wanted to do a parade in Houston at 2 p.m. on a Friday. Hakeem told them he could not attend the parade at that time because he had to pray Al-Jumuah prayer. The team didn't want to do it without him because he was their leader. The parade waited for him in the street and the city waited for him, too. When he finished praying salat Al-Jumu'ah, he joined the parade. They had a good victory parade. Hakeem is my role model.

CHAPTER REVIEW

ACTIVITY TIME

Write a profile about your role model, like the ones you have just read. Share what you wrote with your class. Listen to what they wrote, too. On the board, make a list with your class about what makes a great role model.

Healthy habit

Only choose great Muslim people as your role models. They teach you how to please Allah and do good things.

Study questions

1. What does a role model mean? What's the Arabic word for role model?

2. What do real role models make you do?

3. Name some of the role models mentioned in this lesson.

4. Who are your role models? Why?

5. If you were a role model, what would you do?

UNIT E CHAPTER 2
I Am a Muslim... I Am Honest

questions?

1. How does it feel when someone lies to you?
2. How would you feel if someone stole your money?
3. What does honesty mean?
4. Are you an honest person?
5. Have you been dishonest with anyone before?

word watch

sidq	صِدق
amanah	أمانة
sadiq	صادق
ameen	أمين

Think... Pair... Share...

Think about how it feels to be honest and how it feels to be dishonest. Pair up with someone in your class and share your thoughts.

A Muslim should always practice honesty, or **sidq** صِدق.
He or she speaks the truth and does not lie.
He or she is also trustworthy.
He or she can be trusted with money, things, and secrets.

Q: Do you know who was called
"The Truthful, the Trustworthy" الصادق الأمين ?
If your answer is "Prophet Muhammad ﷺ," you are correct.

People trusted Muhammad ﷺ because he never lied and never cheated anyone. People in Makkah used to give him their expensive things so he could keep them safe. If they told him a secret, he would never tell other people about it. Prophet Muhammad ﷺ had the best manners, just like the Qur'an said about him:

﴿ وَإِنَّكَ لَعَلَىٰ خُلُقٍ عَظِيمٍ ﴾ القلم: ٤

Wa innaka la'ala khuluqin atheem
"And indeed, you are of a great moral character."
Al-Qalam: ayah 4

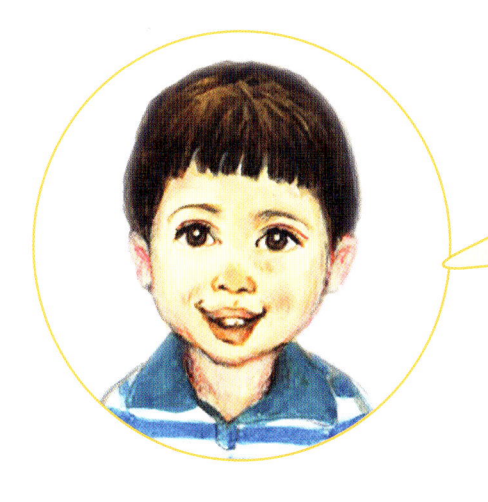

Prophet Muhammad ﷺ taught us to always be honest.
He said:

"عليكم بالصِّدق"

Alaykum Bissidq
"Be honest!"

Allah Sees Us

One night, Omar ibn Al-Khattab, the second Muslim Khaleefah, was walking through the city of Madinah. He was checking on people to look for those who needed help, and to visit the ill.

Then, Omar heard a woman talking to her daughter.

Mother: Dear Daughter, get the milk ready to sell for tomorrow. Since we don't have a lot of milk, mix it with water. That way, we will get more money.

Daughter: But Mother, didn't the Khaleefah Omar forbid cheating?

Mother: Mix it, Dear. Omar cannot see us now.

Daughter: Omar cannot see us now, but Allah can see us all the time.

Khaleefah Omar was very happy with the girl. She was honest and refused to cheat.

Later on, she married Omar's son Asim. She was the grandmother of Omar ibn Abdul Aziz, one of the greatest Muslim khaleefahs ever.

﴿ إِنَّ ٱللَّهَ كَانَ عَلَيْكُمْ رَقِيبًا ﴾ النساء: ١

InnAllaha kana alaykum raqeeba

"Surely, Allah ever watches over you."

Al-Nisa': ayah 1

I Found the Watch

One day Ahmad was feeling very sad. When his friends asked him why, he said he had lost his watch. His grandfather had given him that watch on Eid. His friends helped him look for the watch. They looked in the classroom and the schoolyard, but they found nothing.

Ahmad's friend, Omar, taught him the du'aa that you say when you lose something:

اللهمّ يا جامع الناس ليوم لا ريب فيه، رُدَّ عَلَيّ ضالّتي

"Allahuma ya jami'a-nnasi liyawmin la rayba feeh, rudda alayya dallatee"

"Oh Allah, Who will gather people for a day that there is no doubt about [the Day of Judgment], return to me what I have lost."

Ahmad thanked Omar for teaching him the du'aa.

The next day, Bilal was swinging, and he noticed a shiny object in the sand. He got off the swing and picked it up. It turned out to be Ahmad's missing watch!

Bilal liked the watch very much and said, "This is one cool watch." Although Bilal liked it a lot, he remembered how happy he was when someone returned his lost key chain to him. He knew that honesty makes everyone happy.

Bilal rushed to his teacher and gave her the watch. The teacher returned the watch to Ahmad. Ahmad thanked Bilal for returning his watch. With a smile on his face, Bilal said, "Don't mention it; it was the right thing to do."

Teacher Hibah and his classmates respected him for being honest. She said "Takbeer" for Bilal! Everyone said "Allahu Akbar!"

Why should you be honest?

Honesty brings you closer to Allah سبحانه وتعالى.
Honesty will earn you the trust of people.
Honesty makes everyone respect you.

We have learned:

1. Allah knows everything we say and do.
2. Allah loves those who are honest.
3. Being honest makes everyone happy.
4. When you lose something, say the du'aa.
5. When you are honest, you make others do the same.
6. Prophet Muhammad ﷺ was the best example of honesty.
7. Honesty will lead to Jannah.
8. Honesty will earn you the trust of your parents and others.

Do you want to be a winner?

Be honest!

WORDS OF WISDOM
HADEETH SHAREEF

حديث شريف

Narrated By At-Tirmithi

عن أبي هريرة رضي الله عنه: قال رسول الله ﷺ :

"مَن غَشَّ فَلَيسَ مِنّا" رواه الترمذي

TRANSLITERATION
Man ghasha falaysa minna

TRANSLATION
Abu Hurayrah reported that Prophet Muhammad ﷺ said, "A dishonest person who cheats is not one of us."

CHAPTER REVIEW

Study questions ??

1. What is honesty?
2. What was the nickname of Prophet Muhammad ﷺ?
3. Why is it good to be honest and truthful?
4. Why is it bad to be dishonest and a liar?
5. Why did Khaleefah Omar respect the young woman in the story?
6. Why did everybody in the class say "Allahu Akbar?"

UNIT E CHAPTER 3

I Love My Family

questions?

1. Why is it important to be good to your family?
2. How can you help out people in your family?
3. How should you treat your brothers or sisters?
4. How should you treat your parents?

It was a beautiful Saturday. Mama walked from Zaid's bedroom to Leena's bedroom, waking them up.

"Zaid, Leena, time to wake up!" she called.

Zaid and Leena were still sleepy. But they obeyed Mama and got out of bed. Zaid remembered how long Leena took in the bathroom. He RAN down the hallway to get there before her!

Oh, no! Zaid was too late. Leena got to the bathroom. So Zaid decided he would be patient and wait his turn.

Healthy habit

Always be patient with your brothers and sisters. Help each other learn how to be patient and wait your turn.

Leena was brushing her teeth in the bathroom. She looked carefully at her watch. She did not want to make Zaid wait too long. She knew it was important to care about her brother's feelings.

Soon, Leena came out of the bathroom.
"Assalamu alaykum, Zaid! Good morning."
Zaid was surprised. Leena came out fast today!
"Wow, I didn't wait so long. Thanks, Leena!"
Leena said, "Well, I know you don't like to wait, so I wanted to be quick."
Zaid said, "And I tried to be as patient as I could, too!"

Leena and Zaid had a fight last week. They both had decided to be patient and nicer to each other. Alhamdulillah, it was working.

They went downstairs to have breakfast together. Dad was playing with Baby Yousuf and Mama was fixing breakfast. Leena and Zaid went to hug Dady and Yousuf. They sat down to play with him, but Leena remembered something important.

She said, "Zaid, maybe we should go see if Mama needs our help!"
"Yeah! You're right! Let's go!"
They went to the kitchen.
Together they said, "Assalamu alaykum, Mama, do you need our help?"
Mama smiled, "Wa Alaykum Assalam, Kids! Yes, could you set the table, please?"

After the table was set, the family said "Bismillah" and started eating breakfast.

Dad said, "Mariam, this is a really good breakfast!"
Zaid agreed, "Yeah, Mama! It's the best!"
Leena nodded, because she still had food in her mouth.
Dad said, "Let's hurry up and clean up with Mama, because I think it's a perfect day to go to the park!"
"YAY!" said Zaid and Leena.

They all finished breakfast, and said "Alhamdulillah." The whole family cleaned the table, washed the dishes, and got ready to leave for the park!

They all sat in the car and Zaid reminded them of the du'aa to travel. He loved his family very much. He wanted all of them to do good deeds, so they could all go to Jannah. Zaid also knew it was important to be good to his parents, because Rasulullah had ordered Muslims to do so.

Healthy habit

Always help your parents whenever they need help.

WORDS OF WISDOM
HADEETH SHAREEF

حديث شريف

Narrated By Ibn Majah & At-Tirmithi

عن عباس رضي الله عنه: قال رسول الله ﷺ:

"خَيْرُكُم خَيْرُكُم لِأَهْلِهِ وَأَنا خَيْرُكُم لِأَهْلي" رواه ابن ماجه والترمذي

TRANSLITERATION

"Khayrukum khayrukum li'ahlih, wa ana khayrukum li'ahli"

TRANSLATION

Ibn Abbas رضي الله عنه reported that the Prophet ﷺ said, "The best among you is he who is good to his family, and I am the best of you to my family."

Healthy habit

Listen to your parents as soon as they tell you to do something. This shows that you love them.

While they were driving to the park, Dad was telling funny jokes. Leena and Zaid laughed so hard, their stomachs felt funny!

Baby Yousuf heard all the noise and started crying.
Zaid said, "Uh, oh!"
Leena said, "Baby Yousuf, don't cry!"
They both loved their baby brother very much and stopped making the noise so he could feel better.

When they got to the park, Zaid ran to help Mama carry the picnic basket. Leena helped Dad take out the balls. They wanted to help their parents because they loved them a lot.

They walked in the park together for a little while, then picked a nice spot to put their stuff down.

Mama and Dad watched Baby Yousuf crawl around, doing funny things.

Leena and Zaid ran to the playground, laughing together. They played on the seesaw, they sat on the swings, and they took turns on the slide!

Then it was time to eat lunch. Mama called her children to come back, "Zaid! Leena! It's time for lunch!" Zaid and Leena listened to their mother and ran back to their parents.

Leena and Zaid kissed their baby brother because he was so cute. They couldn't wait until he was big enough to play with them! Lunch was ready, and the Mahmood family began to eat.

There was only one cookie left after dessert. Leena and Zaid both wanted to eat it! Chocolate chip cookies were their favorite. Then Leena remembered that her parents and teachers always taught her to share what she loved. She said to Zaid, "You can have the cookie, Zaid. I love you."

Zaid was very happy, but he loved his sister, too!
Zaid said, "No, Leena, I changed my mind. You can eat it."

Mama was very happy with her children.

Mama said, "I have an idea! Why don't you share the cookie? Zaid can have half, and Leena can have half!"
Zaid and Leena started eating the cookie.

When they were ready to leave, Zaid and Leena hugged their parents and said, "Thank you, Jazakum Allah khairan," for taking them to the park.
Baba said, "We love you, and we are proud that you are such great kids. That is why we wanted to reward you by bringing you here!"

Mama, Dad, Zaid, Leena, and Baby Yousuf had a fun day together. They loved each other very much. They always helped each other and made each other feel good and happy. To show how much they loved each other, they shared, helped, and listened to each other as much as they could.

CHAPTER REVIEW

ACTIVITY TIME

1. Make a list of things you should do to make your family love you.

2. Make another list of things you should avoid because they make your parents or family upset with you.

Study questions

1. What did the Prophet ﷺ say about how to treat our families?

2. How was Zaid patient in the morning? How was Leena nice in the morning?

3. Did Leena and Zaid listen to Mama? When?

4. What were some other nice things the kids did for their parents?

5. What was the nice thing Dad did for the family?

6. How were Zaid and Leena nice to Baby Yousuf?

7. Who got to eat the cookie? Why?

UNIT E CHAPTER 4
I Respect My Teachers and Elders

questions?

1. Why should you respect your teacher?
2. Why do teachers and elders set rules?
3. What might happen if you disobey your teacher?

word watch

Ta'ah طاعة
(Obedience)

It was a very pretty day, and Bilal was on a field trip with his class to the zoo. Teacher Hibah was telling them about the different animals. Bilal was having fun learning and watching the tigers. He was glad that his teacher taught him so many wonderful things.

When the class sat down for lunch, Bilal sat with his friends. Zaid was not there because he was sick. Bilal missed his best friend. As Bilal was eating his sandwich, Amir and his friends came up to him.

Amir: Hey, Bilal!
Bilal: Assalamu Alaykum, Amir.
Amir: We finished eating already, and we're going to go look at the alligators. Do you want to come with us?
Bilal: But the class is still eating! You know we're not allowed to go alone!
Amir: Come on, it won't take very long. We will be back soon.
Bilal thought to himself: Amir was not asking him to do a good thing. Teacher Hibah had always taught the class to obey the rules and do good things.

Besides, Teacher Hibah had told them this morning, "Stay with your class the whole time, kids. I want you all to be safe."

So Bilal told Amir: I'm not coming with you, Amir. I will obey Teacher Hibah's rules. You shouldn't go, either. We have to show ta'ah, obedience to our teachers and elders.
Amir answered: Well, Teacher Hibah will never know. We will be back soon.
Bilal: Allah will know that you broke the rules. And He will know that you disobeyed our teacher. Teacher Hibah just wants us to be safe. She was nice to bring us to the zoo and teach us about the animals. We should respect her kindness.
Amir: Well, you can stay here. We're still going.

Amir ran off with his friends when Teacher Hibah wasn't looking. Bilal was sad that his classmates were not being good.

Pretty soon, the class was ready to go look at more animals.
Teacher Hibah: Okay class, clean up and let's have some more fun!
Bilal got worried. Amir and the boys were not back yet.
Teacher Hibah saw that the class looked smaller.
Teacher Hibah: Who's missing? Where are Amir, Khalid, and Omar?
Bilal did not want something bad to happen. He said, "Teacher Hibah, they went to go look at the alligators."
Teacher Hibah did not look happy at all.
She said: They were not supposed to go anywhere alone! We have to find them now!

E33

The class was not smiling, either. Now they could not see more animals and have more fun until the boys were found. They looked everywhere, and the boys were still lost. They even looked by the alligators. Now everyone was worried.

Mona: Where did they go? What if something happened to them?

Teacher Hibah: Insha'Allah they are safe. But this is why you are not allowed to leave the group.

Then, far away, they saw the zookeeper walking toward them with three little boys in front of him.
Bilal: There they are!

Bilal saw that Amir and his friends looked very scared.

Zookeeper: Are these boys with your class?
Teacher Hibah: Yes, they are. Thank you for bringing them back. Where were they?
Zookeeper: They were lost, and they asked me to help them find your class.

Teacher Hibah was very upset.
Teacher Hibah: Boys, do you know how worried I was? The class was worried too! You will have to be punished for breaking the rules. I will call your parents, and no more field trips for you boys.

Amir, Khalid, and Omar looked ashamed. They knew that they had done a bad thing, and now they were in big trouble.
Amir, Khalid, Omar: We are very sorry for everything, Teacher Hibah. We will try to be good and obey you from now on.

E35

Sorry!

Healthy habit

Always say sorry if you do something wrong, and learn from your mistakes. Don't do them again.

Teacher Hibah: Well, it is time to go back to school now. I hope you boys learned your lesson. Teachers and parents make rules that are good for you.

Amir: Oh, we did learn our lesson! We didn't even get to see the alligators, we made everyone worried and sad, and now we are in big trouble! I wish I had listened to you, Teacher. Then everything would have been okay.

Elders set rules to keep you safe.

Bilal went up to Amir: When we listen to our teacher, we make Allah سبحانه وتعالى happy. When we disobey her, then we need to ask Allah سبحانه وتعالى and our teacher for forgiveness.

Amir: I'm sorry I did not listen to you before, Bilal. You were telling me the right thing to do.

Bilal: It's okay, Amir. Let's just help each other be good.

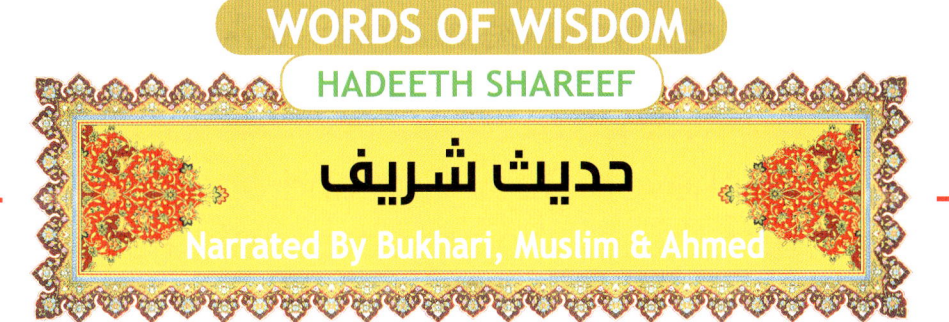

WORDS OF WISDOM
HADEETH SHAREEF

حديث شريف

Narrated By Bukhari, Muslim & Ahmed

عن أبي هريرة رضي الله عنه: قال رسول الله ﷺ :

"اسمعوا وأطيعوا واصبروا" رواه البخاري ومسلم وأحمد

TRANSLITERATION

"Isma'oo wa-atee'oo wasbiroo"

TRANSLATION

Abu Hurayra reported that the Prophet ﷺ said, "Listen (to your elders); obey and be patient."

WORDS OF WISDOM
HOLY QUR'AN

سورة النساء

Surat An-Nisa': ayah 59

بِسْمِ ٱللَّهِ ٱلرَّحْمَٰنِ ٱلرَّحِيمِ

﴿ يَٰٓأَيُّهَا ٱلَّذِينَ ءَامَنُوٓا۟ أَطِيعُوا۟ ٱللَّهَ وَأَطِيعُوا۟ ٱلرَّسُولَ وَأُو۟لِى ٱلْأَمْرِ مِنكُمْ ﴾

TRANSLITERATION

"Ya ayyuha allatheena aamanoo atteeoo Allaha wa atteeoo arrasoola wa olee alamri minkum"

TRANSLATION

"O you who believe! Obey God and obey the Messenger and those who are responsible of you."

Healthy habit

Always be obedient to your parents and teachers. Follow the rules they set for you.

CHAPTER REVIEW

ACTIVITY TIME

With your friends, make a play about obeying parents and teachers and act it out in front of your class.

Study questions?

1. What did Amir ask Bilal to do at lunchtime?

2. Why did Bilal stay with the class?

3. What happened to Amir and his friends?

4. Why did Teacher Hibah set the rule for the children to stay with the class?

5. Do you think Allah was happy with Amir, Khalid, and Omar? How can you keep Allah happy?

6. Did Bilal do the right thing by telling the teacher that Amir had left?

UNIT E CHAPTER 5

Zaid and Leena Go to the Masjid

questions?

1. Why do Muslims go to the masjid?
2. Do you go to the masjid? What do you do there?
3. How many times should we visit the masjid every day?
4. Do you like going to the masjid? Why?

word watch

halaqah حَلقة
jama'ah جماعة
thikr ذِكْر
Jumu'ah جُمُعة

The masjid is a peaceful place to pray, make du'aa, make thikr, and to read Al-Qur'an. **Thikr** is when we remember Allah and say His name.

- A beautiful masjid from inside.

- The masjid in Tempe, Arizona, with a dome and minaret. It looks like Qubbat Al-Sakhrah in Jerusalem.

E41

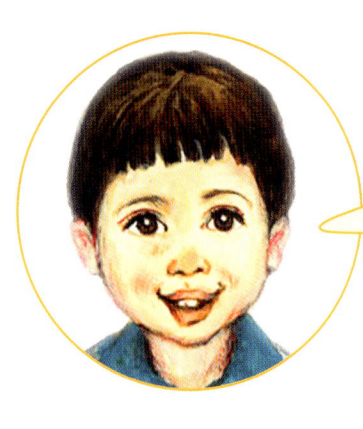

Dad takes us to the masjid almost every day!

We've been going to the masjid since we were babies!

Healthy habit

Rasulullah told us to say this du'aa every time you enter the masjid:

اللهم افتح لي أبواب رحمتك

"Allahumma iftah li abwaaba rahmatik"
This means: "O Allah, open Your doors of mercy for me." (Muslim)

IT IS SUNNAH TO ENTER THE MASJID WITH YOUR RIGHT FOOT!

Mama and I take Zaid and Leena to the masjid whenever we can, so they can become good Muslims. A Muslim should try to go to the masjid for every prayer.

The whole family loves going to the masjid because we enjoy **jama'ah** prayer, and there are so many things to do there!

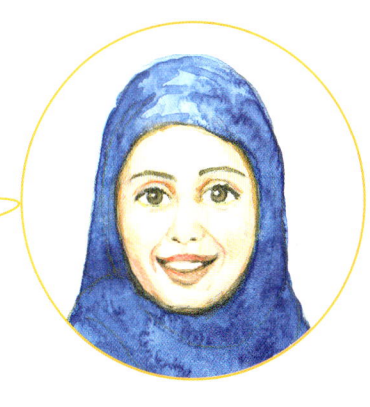

I learn so many things in the halaqah we have at the masjid! In the **halaqah**, we sit together and talk about Islam. Last week, we learned about fasting.

I love to pray in **jama'ah**, together with all my Muslim brothers! I get much more reward when I pray with the jama'ah in the masjid.

WORDS OF WISDOM
HADEETH SHAREEF

حديث شريف

Narrated By Bukhari & Muslim

عن أبي هريرة رضي الله عنه: قال رسول الله ﷺ :

"مَنْ غدا إلى المسجد أو راح أَعَدَّ اللهُ له في الجَنَّة نُزُلاً كلما غدا أو راح"

رواه البخاري ومسلم

TRANSLITERATION

Man ghada ilal masjidi aw rah , a'add-Allahu lahu fil jannati nuzulan kullama ghada aw rah.

TRANSLATION

The Prophet ﷺ said, "For whomever goes to the mosque then he returns home, God will build a house in Paradise every time he goes and returns."

E45

So many Muslims come to Jumu'ah prayers every week! **Jumu'ah** prayers are at Thuhr time every Friday. It is our special prayer.

E47

Healthy habit

There is a great reward for those who clean the masjid, even if they remove a little dirt from it. Always keep the masjid clean and shiny so everyone enjoys it.

One day, there were children running around and making noise in the prayer hall. I knew this would disturb people's prayers, so I stayed quiet and told my friends to do the same thing. We can always play in other places.

The masjid is for us to pray, NOT to play!

Healthy habit

Rasulullah told us to say this du'aa every time you leave the masjid:

اللهم إني أسألك من فضلك

"Allahumma inni as-aluka min fadhlik"

This means, "O Allah, I ask you for your grace and your blessings." (Muslim)

CHAPTER REVIEW

Study questions

1. What are three things you can do in a masjid?

2. What are the du'aa for entering and leaving the masjid?

3. What is the special weekly prayer for Muslims? When do we pray it?

4. The masjid makes us good Muslims, because we can be closer to Allah when we pray there. We also learn at the masjid. What is something nice you can do to take care of the masjid?

E49

UNIT E CHAPTER 6

Learning Is First

questions?

1. What should you say before traveling anywhere?
2. Why is it good to be patient?
3. How should we treat our Muslim brothers and sisters?

word watch

Du'aa Ar-Rukoob دعاء الركوب

Leena heard the call of the Fajr athan and stretched her arms and legs. Then she remembered that today was a special day! Today Mama was going to take all her friends to the big new mall! Leena needed to buy a book, and Mama was giving them all a treat! Leena hurried out of bed to pray and eat breakfast.

As soon as they were ready, Leena and her mother left the house. They read the du'aa of leaving the house.

بِسْمِ اللهِ، تَوَكَّلْنَا عَلَى اللهِ، لَا حَوْلَ وَلَا قُوَّةَ إِلَّا بِاللهِ

"Bismillah, tawakkalna 'ala-llah, la hawla, wa la quwwata, illah billah."

"In the name of Allah, we rely on Him, and we will not have power or strength without Allah's support."

Then they sat in the car to go pick up her friends. Mama and Leena also did not forget to say **Du'aa Ar-Rukoob** (travel prayer) together.

سُبْحَانَ الَّذِي سَخَّرَ لَنَا هَذَا وَمَا كُنَّا لَهُ مُقْرِنِينَ، وَإِنَّا إِلَى رَبِّنَا لَمُنْقَلِبُونَ

"Subhan-allathi sakhara lana hatha wa ma kunna lahu muqrineen, wa inna ila rabbina la munqaliboon."

"Glory is to Him Who has provided this for us, though we could never have had it by our efforts. Surely, unto our Lord we are returning."

Abu Dawood and At-Tirmithi

Healthy habit

Always read du'aa of leaving the home when you step out of your house. Read the du'aa of riding when you sit in a car or something else you travel in.

E51

Their first stop was Sarah's house. She came running out of her house to the car.

"Assalamu alaykum, Auntie Mariam and Leena!"
"Wa alaykum assalaam," said both Leena and her mother.
"How are you, Auntie?" asked Sarah.
"Alhamdulillah, Dear. How is your mother?" answered Mariam.
"She's doing well, Alhamdulillah."

Sarah and Leena were so excited because they were going to have so much fun! Next came Aminah's house. As soon as she was in the car, they were on their way to the mall!

They came closer and closer, and soon they saw a big building.

"Masha'Allah!" All the girls said. The mall was so big! Leena's mother parked the car, and they all got out.
"Remember, Girls: we need to stay together in this big place. I don't want any of you to get lost," she told them. The girls listened to Auntie Mariam and held hands.

E53

They entered the mall, and all the girls froze! There was an amusement park inside the mall!

"SURPRISE!" said Leena's mother. "Since you all have been doing so well in school, all the parents wanted to give you a treat!"

The girls were really surprised, and very happy. They wanted to run to the rides and start the fun!
"Oh!" said Leena. "I forgot what we even came here for! I need to buy my book first, right Mama?"
Leena's mother replied, "I am very proud of you for remembering, My Dear. I forgot, too! This mall is so pretty! But we should always remember what is important first. Learning is always before fun."
"I hope Allah will reward us for being patient and putting knowledge first! What are we waiting for? Let's go!" said Leena.

They entered the bookstore and started looking for the book they needed. Leena found her book quickly and got in line to pay for it with her friends and mother. It was a very long line. They looked out the window and saw all the other children having fun in the amusement park.

"That sure looks like fun!" said Sarah.
 "I wish we didn't have to wait!" said Leena. The line began to take so long!
"I know, but good things come to people who are patient."

Healthy h a b i t

Always be patient, and put important things first.

While they were talking, the line grew shorter. Soon, it was Leena's turn, and she bought the book. It was finally time to go to the amusement park!

The first ride they got to was the bumper cars. Aminah got to the pink car first, but all the girls wanted the pink one. There was only room for one person in it!

"Mama, but I wanted the pink one!" whispered Leena.
"Aminah is your good friend, isn't she darling?"
"Well. . .yes," answered Leena.
"As Muslims, we should love for other Muslims what we love for ourselves. It will make Allah happy."

Aminah heard Leena's mother telling her this and

stopped before she sat down. She wanted to be a good Muslim, too! "Leena, you can have my car. I will sit in the purple one instead." Leena had a big smile on her face. It was very nice of her friend to offer the pink car to her.

"Thank you so much, Aminah, but it's okay! I'll sit in the blue car. It will be fun either way!"

"Let's go!" cried Sarah. "Yippeeeee!"

WORDS OF WISDOM
HADEETH SHAREEF

حديث شريف

Narrated By At-Tirmithi & Ahmad

عن أبي هريرة رضي الله عنه: قال رسول الله ﷺ :

"مَنْ لا يَشْكُرِ النَّاسَ لا يَشْكُرِ اللهَ" رواه الترمذي وأحمد

TRANSLITERATION

"Man La Yashkuri-nnas La Yashkurillah"

TRANSLATION

Abu Hurayrah reported that the Prophet ﷺ said, "He who does not thank people does not thank God."

The girls had fun on the bumper cars and all the other rides. They remembered to be nice to each other. All that mattered was that they were all having fun together!

On the way home, the girls remembered how they learned to be patient and caring. They did important things before they had fun. Then they remembered one last thing.

"THANK YOU, AUNTIE MARIAM!"

Healthy habit

When you go to the mall or the market say:

لا إله إلا الله وحده لا شريك له، له الملك وله الحمد يحيي ويميت وهو حي لا يموت بيده الخير وهو على كل شيء قدير

La ilaha illa Allah wahdahu la shareeka lah, lahu-lmulk wa lahulhamd, yuhyee wa yumeet, wa huwa hayyun la yamoot, biyadih-il-khayr, wa huwa ala kulli shay'in qadeer. It means: " There is no god but Allah alone, He has no partner, He has the majesty and praise, He gives life and death, He is alive and does not die, and He can do anything."

CHAPTER REVIEW

Study questions

1. What is the du'aa for traveling?
2. How do Muslims greet one another?
3. What should you do first: something important such as learning, or something fun?
4. Should you think of yourself or your Muslim friend first?

UNIT E CHAPTER 7

My Muslim Room

questions?

1. Why should you keep your room clean?
2. What kind of problems can you have if you have a messy room?
3. Do you keep your room nice and clean?
4. Whom do you please if you keep your room nice and clean?
5. Who is responsible for keeping your room clean and neat?

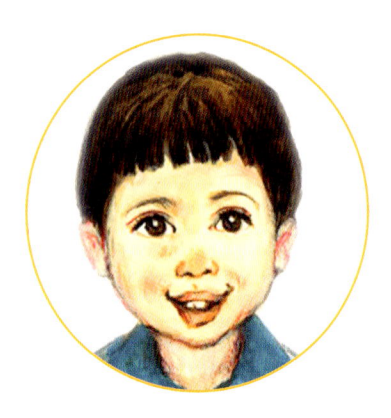

One weekend, Zaid went to Amir's house for lunch. He knew that he was going to have fun playing with his friend!

Zaid: Assalamu Alaykum, Amir!
Amir: Wa Alaykum Assalaam, Zaid! Let's play!
Amir's Mom: You boys have to eat your lunch first. Welcome, Zaid.
Zaid: Thank you, Auntie.

So Zaid and Amir washed their hands, said the du'aa before eating, then ate some yummy sandwiches and drank juice.

Then they washed their hands again and ran to Amir's room to play.

Zaid tripped and fell as he ran into Amir's room. He looked around to see what had made him fall. He saw a toy truck sitting in the doorway.
Amir: Sorry about that, Zaid. Are you okay?
Zaid: Yeah, I'm okay. Alhamdulillah.

He looked around at Amir's room. It was a big mess! There were clothes, toys, and books on the floor. Trash was everywhere! Zaid thought he smelled something funny.

E61

Zaid moved some things around and found a place to sit.
Amir: Do you want to play my new adventure board game? It's fun.
Zaid: Yeah!

Amir reached under his bed for the game, but found nothing.
Amir: That's funny, I thought I put it right here!
Amir hopped over his toys and clothes to his closet. He opened the closet door and clothes and toys fell out!
Amir: It must be in here.

Amir started throwing the clothes over his shoulder, looking for the game. One of his socks landed on Zaid's head. Zaid hoped it was a clean sock.

Amir couldn't find his game in the closet, either.

Amir: It must be in my drawers!

He started to go through his drawers, pulling out more stuff. He found a banana peel and he pinched his nose. There was the funny smell!

Still no game!

Zaid waited patiently for his friend. Amir was getting tired of searching so hard. He sat down hard on the ground, and there was a loud crunch!

Amir sat down right on the adventure game! He couldn't see it because it was covered with a shirt. Zaid started to laugh.

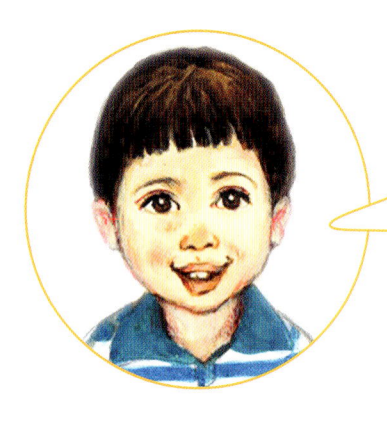

"I guess you found your game, Amir!"

Amir laughed, too. "It was right here the whole time! I just couldn't see it!"

Zaid thought to himself, "If Amir's room were clean, then we would have a much better time playing." And he knew that Allah loves it when children keep their things nice and clean.

Healthy habit

Keep your room nice and clean, put everything in the right place, and help others do the same. This makes Allah happy.

Zaid: Hey, Amir! you know what we should do to have more fun?

Amir: What?

Zaid: We could clean your room and then sit down on the floor to play the game! Right now I don't think we have room.

Amir: I think you're right. Let's do it!

Amir started putting his clothes away nicely, while Zaid picked up the toys and books. They both picked up the trash and put it all in the basket. Then they made Amir's bed, and Amir even brought a vacuum to finish up.

When they were all done, the room looked very, very nice.

Zaid: You have a really cool room, Amir.

Amir: Yes, Alhamdulillah I have a nice room. I should always keep it clean. A Muslim's room should always be clean and neat. You helped me a lot, Zaid. Thanks!

Zaid: I want to give you a gift for your room. It will make it look even better.

Amir: Really? What is that?

Zaid: A beautiful poster of Al-Ka'bah! I have two at home.

Amir: Jazakum Allahu khairan, Zaid. That will be great.

Zaid: You're welcome, Amir.

Healthy habit

Have nice Islamic posters on your room's wall. It will make your room pretty and remind you of something good.

E67

Zaid and Amir didn't see Amir's mom come into the room. She was amazed to see such a clean room!

Amir's Mom: Wow, Amir! You finally cleaned up your room! I could have cleaned it for you, but I wanted you to learn to take care of your room all by yourself. Keep it clean, and Allah will be happy with you, just like I am very happy with you!

Amir: Zaid helped me, Mom. Thanks again, Zaid.

Zaid: Anytime, Amir!

Healthy habit

Always give advice to your friend in a nice way.

CHAPTER REVIEW

ACTIVITY TIME

When you go home today, make your room the cleanest and neatest in the whole house! Then, help your other family members clean their rooms if they need it.

Study questions

1. Why couldn't Amir find his game?

2. Why did Zaid fall down?

3. Who was happy with Amir when his room was clean?

4. Do you think Allah was happy with Zaid for helping his friend?

5. How should you keep your room?

INDEX

A

Aam-ul-Fee B1-2
Abdul-Muttalib B2, B5-7, B11, B14-15, B22, B26, B29-30, B35
Abdullah B14-15, B52, B56, B75
Abraha B2, B4-7, B9, B11
Abu Talib B34-45, B37-38, B43
Adam A1-3, A7-8, A10-11, A15-17, A24, A29, A38-39
Ahadeeth C2, C6
air B17, B35
Aisha C7
Al Imran A68
Al-Abbas B68-69
Al-Aleem A62, A64
Al-Atheem A30
Al-Awwal A18, A23
Al-Baseer A62, A64
Al-Ghaffar A10
Al-Ghafoor A10
Al-Hajar Al-Aswad B42, B44-45, B49, B51, B59
Al-Hasan B68-B70
Al-Hussayn B68-70
Al-Ka'bah B2-8, B11, B13, B19, B44, B49-51
Al-Khabeer A62, A64
Al-Mu'awwithat C2, C4
Al-Mughni B29
Al-Qasim B52, B56
Al-Waseelah B76
Alhamdulillah B32, B56
alive A35
Allahu Akbar A35
alone A62-63, A66, A68, B20, B24, B28, B39
Aminah B12, B14-16, B21, B24, B75
angel A2-3, A7-8, A15, A17, B20, C2, C6
angry A4, A26, A32-33, A35, A50, A54, B4
animal A39, A43, A45, B34-35, B42
ant A43, A62
apples A65-66, A73
Arabia B2-3, B16, B38, B41
Arabic A23, B2, B17, C3
Arabs B4

ark A38, A41-45, A47
army B5, B7, B9
arrogant A3
As-Sadiq Al-Ameen B1, B42-43, B45
As-Samee' A55, A62
Asia A36
Assalamu alaykum B43
Astaghfirullah A9
athan A19, C1
attack B6
axe A32
ayaat A46, A58, C6
ayah A4, A9, A31, A54, A62, A66, A68
Azar A32

B

Baghdad A36, A57
Baheera B37-38
barakah B22
believer A21, A45, A60, B77
bird A28, B7, B10, B71
Bismillah A18, A21, A67-68
Black Stone B44-45, B49-51
blessed B1, B34, B36, B75
boat A41, A51
book C2, C5-6, C9
born A37, B16, B19, B75, C1
bow A3, A15
brother A24-28, B21
burn A4, A35
bury A28
Busra B37

C

camels B5-6, B41, B49, B69
capital A36
caravan B37, B40-41, B49
children A11, A24, A38, A67, B1, B23, B25, B29, B43, B46, B52, B57, B68-69, B77
Christian B37
church B4, B37
city A72
clay A2-3, B10
clean A22, B17-18, B75
clothes A11, A15, C4

cloud B37
command A38, A45, A47, B7, C9
companion B70, C6
cool A35
country A36, B2, B4
cousins B69
creator A1, A30, A41, B39
creatures A3, B29, C9
crime A27
cupcake A67-68
cursed A4-5

D
dark A48, A52
darkness A52, A54, B28
dates B15
daughter B14, B56
days A45, A50, A54
Day of Judgment A59, B31
dead A28, A39
deed A4, A18, A20, A23, A40, A72, C9
desert A73, B17, B21, B23, B61
die A35, B15-16, B24, B30, B32, B41, B56, B71, B77
disobey A3-4, A8, A11, A15, A17, A44, A47, A61
drown A41, A44
du'aa A19, A48, A54-55, A57, A60, B28, C1, C4-5
dying A31

E
Earth A10-11, A24, A27, A38-39, A45, A47, A62-63, A68, B3, B48
eat A7-8, A18, A67
elephant A43, B1-2, B5-7, B10-11, B13-14
enemy A12, A15, A17
English B2
Eternity A15, C9
Euphrates A36
Eve A7
evidence C9
evil A15, A72, B10
eyes A47, A72

F
Fajr C5
faith B6, C9
family A24, A37, A67, B14, B17-18, B22-24, B31, B35, B49, B52, B54-55, B61
father A2, A23, A31-32, A44, B16, B19, B21, B24-25, B38, C4-5
Fatimah B52, B56
fear A28, B40
female A43
fight B5, B44
fire A3, A35, A72
flood A41, B44, B49
food A7, A11, A15, A39, A72, B17, B23
forbidden A8
forever A7-8, C9
forgive A8-11, A17, A57, A61
forgiveness A9, A53-54
friend A12-13, A29, A65-66, B18, B21, B30, B55, B66, B72-73
fruit A7-8

G
Garden A15, C9
gate A47, B49
gift B28, B61
grandfather A67-68, A73, B24, B26, B29-30, B32, B35, B41
grandmother A67
grandsons B68, B77
grass A22
graves B65
guidance A15, C5

H
Habeel A24-25, A28-29
Hadeeth A21, B76-77, C2, C5-7
Haleemah B12, B17-18, B22-24
harm A32, B6
Hasanat A23, C3
Hawwaa' A7
healthy habit A5, A9, A17, A21, A27, A29, A35, A54-55, A60, B13, B17, B21, B26, B28, B31, B36, B48, B53, B65, B74, C3
hear A32, A62, A64, A73

E71

INDEX

heat A15
Heaven A4, A47, A62-63, A68, B48
Hell A4, A27, C9
help A39, A60, B28, C4
herds B5
Hereafter B28
hero A28, A35
hide A67
hills B6
home A56, A65, A67, B28, B38
honest B36, B43, B46, B48, B53, B55, B72
human A2-3, A17
hungry A15, A32
hurt A29, A52, A69, B7, B26
husband B15, B54

I

Iblees A2-4, A14-15
Ibraheem A30-33, A35-37, B3
idol A32-33, A37, A39-40, B34, B39
Iman A1, B2, B6, C5
Insha'Allah A23, B30, B46, B72
intention A22
Iraq A31, A36-37, A49
Isha C4
Islam A39, A49, A60, B19-20, B59, C2
Isma'eel B3

J

Jannah A2, A7, A11, A48, B76
Jazakum Allahu khairan A66, B34, B36, B46, B57, B72
jealous A25-26, B4
Jibreel C2, C6
Jinn A2-3
journey A56
Judy A38, A45

K

Khadeejah B54-57, B59, B61-62
kill A25, A27-28, A35, A39
kingdom A15

L

land A36, A42, B19, B50
lie A7, B36, B53
life A1, A11, A59, B13, B21, B28
lightning A43
lips A72
listen A2, A11-12, A27, A41, A60-61, B12-13, B44, B56

M

Madinah B71
Maghrib A19, A22
Makkah A72, B2-6, B11, B14-15, B17, B19, B22, B24, B35, B37-38, B41, B61
male A43
marriage B1, B52, B59
marry A24-25, B14, B54-55, B57
masjid A22, B45, C4
Mecca B75
merchant B43, B53, B61
merciful A8, A57
mercy A4, A9
messenger A21, A47, A59, C9
mistake A16-17, A61
money A72, B28, B55
moon A30
mother A2, A19, A22, B19, B21, B24-25, B32, B61, C4
morning B6, B28, B65, B74
mountain A44-45, B39, B41
Muslim A12-13, A26, A29, A36, B20, B25, B31-32, B42, B55-56, B76, C3, C7

N

name A2, A7, A17, A24, A29, B20, B57, B59-60, B66-67, B71, B74, B77
nasheed A12-13, B19-20, B49-50, B57, B75
Naynawa A48-50, A56-57, A60
neighbors A39
night A45, A52, A54, B16, B20, B28
niyyah A18, A22-23
noise A43
Nughair B68, B71, B77
Nuh A1, A38-45, A47

O

obedient A35, B25
obey A1-2, A7, A11, A17, A23-24, A28, A41, A44, A47, A49-50, A57, B6-7, B17, B72-73
ocean A42
Omair B68, B71
Omar ibn-ul-Khattab A69
orphan A72, B1, B19, B22, B24, B28, B30-32, B38
owner B6

P

pagans C9
Paradise A7-8, A11, A38
parent A20, A72, B12, B16-17, B26, B31, B57-58, B62, B66-67, B72-73
path A27, A72
patient A53-55, B31, B56
peace C3
penalty A47
permission A50, A53, A59
playing A18
poem A73, B76
poor A72, B19, B28-29, B31, B35
pray A12-13, A19-20, A30, A39, A57, B6, B25, B70, B72-73, B75, B77, C1, C4, C9
prayer A9, A19, A31, A60, B7, B31
priest B37-38
promise A4, A45
protect A5, A11, A68, B6, B11, B38
punished A4, A40-41, A50, B31
punishment A17, A28, A57
pure B17, C9

Q

Qabeel A24-25, A27-29
Qayn A24
Qur'an A7, A9, A12-14, A31, A46-47, A58, A62, A66, A70, B10, B20, B27, B31, B40, B47, B64, B76, C2-3, C5-8
Quraysh B40, B44, B49, B51, B59
qurban A24-25

R

rain A42-43, A45
Rajeem A2, A4-5
Ramadan C1
Rasulullah A21, B42, B58, B75, C6
read A12, B20, C2-3
relative A39, A72
religion C9
remember A16-17, A20, A22, A26, A47, B13, C7
respect A3, B36, B53, B55-57, B72-73
reward A23, A47, A66, B22, B36, C4, C9
rib A7
river A36, A42, C9
roses B70
Ruqayyah B52, B56

S

sabr A48, A55
sacrifice A25
safe A35, A41, A44, B6, B25, B38, B40
sahabah B68, B70
sahabi B67
salah C1
Satan A4, A15
Saudi Arabia B2-3
saved A45
scriptures C9
sea A38, A51, A61
secrets A69, B65
see A1, A32, A62, A64-67, A73
Seerah B12-13, B21, B34, B42, B46, B52, B59
selfish A25
servant A47-48, B58, B62
Shaytan A2, A4-5, A7-8, A11-14, A17, A25-27, A29
sheep B23
shepherd B35
ship A38, A50-51, A59, A61
shore A56, A59
sick A32, A56, A59, B15, B24
sign A47, A72
sin A15, A69
sincere A11

INDEX

sisters A26, B21
sky A43, A45, B7
slave A72, B61, B67
sleep A7, A18, B74, C4
speak A32
soldiers B5
son A1, A24, A29, A44, A62, B5, B14-15, B35, B56, B69, B75
sorry A11, A57
souls A9
special A20
springs A43, A47
statues A30-31, A33, B39
stomach A52, A54, A56, A61
stones A31-32, B7, B10, B39, B44-45, B50
storm A51, A57
stranger A12
Subhan'Allah A66, B66
sujood B68, B70
summer B40
sun A15, A30, A73, B37
Sunnah B65, B72, C2
Surah B10, B32, B65, C2, C6
Surat Ad-Duha B1, B27, B32
Surat An-Nas C4
Surat Luqman A62
Surat Quraysh B40
Surat Taha A14
Surat Al-'Adiyat B64
Surat Al-A'raf A9
Surat Al-An'aam A31
Surat Al-'Anbiya' A54
Surat Al-Bayyinah C8
Surat Al-Balad A70
Surat Al-Falaq C4
Surat Al-Feel B10
Surat Al-Hijr A4
Surat Al-Ma'un B31
Surat Al-Qamar A46
Surat Al-Saffat A58
Surat Ash-Sharh B47
Surat At-Tawba A66
suwar C2, C6-7

swallow A45, A52, A59
Syria B37, B43, B55

T
taqwa A1, A24, A28, A62, A65-66, A69, A73
tasbeeh A48, A54
thank A20, B30, B35
thikr C1
thirst A15
thorns A69
thunder A43
Tigris A36
tongue A72
town A31, A40, A60, B15, B19
trash A22-23
travel B34, B37
treasures C1-2, C4-6
tree A7-8, A15, A36, A56, A59, A65, A68, A73
trick A4, A8
trust A1, A35, A38, B7, B42, B45-46, B48
trusted B1, B43
truth A44, C9
truthful B1, B43, B55

U
Ummu Kulthum B52, B56
uncle B24, B35, B37, B41, B69
Ur A31

V
village A49-50, A57

W
Wa'iyyakum B46, B57, B72
Waalaykum Assalaam B43
Wahb B14
warning A41, A47
water A44-45, A47, A51-52, B23, B49
weak A26
weapons A11
whale A52, A54, A56, A59, A61
whisper A12-13, A15, A64
wife A7-8, A10-11, A15-16, A24, A44, B14, B52, B55

E74

wind A57
winter B40
woman A7, B21
Words of Wisdom A9, A14, A21, A31, A46, A58, A66, A70, B10, B27, B31, B40, B47, B64, B77, C7-8
work A11, A25, B20, B48, B53-55
world A22, A31, A39, B28, B37, B39, B70
worship A11, A20, A30-32, A37, A39-41, A49, A57, B3, B20, B31, B39-40, C1, C9
wrong A5, A8-9, A27, A53-54
wudoo' C1

Y
Yam A44
Yathrib B12, B15, B24, B41
Yemen B2-4
Younus (ibn Matta) A1, A48-57, A59-61

Z
Zaid Bin Harithah B1, B58, B60, B62, B66-67
zakat C9
Zaynab B52, B56